THE POWER OF GOOSE ISLAND PARK

© Copyright 2005 Ken Crassweller.
All rights reserved. No part of this publication may be reproduced, stored in a retrieval system, or transmitted, in any form or by any means, electronic, mechanical, photocopying, recording, or otherwise, without the written prior permission of the author.

Note for Librarians: A cataloguing record for this book is available from Library and Archives Canada at www.collectionscanada.ca/amicus/index-e.html
ISBN 1-4120-5396-X

Printed in Victoria, BC, Canada. Printed on paper with minimum 30% recycled fibre. Trafford's print shop runs on "green energy" from solar, wind and other environmentally-friendly power sources.

TRAFFORD

Offices in Canada, USA, Ireland and UK
This book was published on-demand in cooperation with Trafford Publishing. On-demand publishing is a unique process and service of making a book available for retail sale to the public taking advantage of on-demand manufacturing and Internet marketing. On-demand publishing includes promotions, retail sales, manufacturing, order fulfilment, accounting and collecting royalties on behalf of the author.

Book sales for North America and international:
Trafford Publishing, 6E–2333 Government St.,
Victoria, BC v8t 4p4 CANADA
phone 250 383 6864 (toll-free 1 888 232 4444)
fax 250 383 6804; email to orders@trafford.com
Book sales in Europe:
Trafford Publishing (uk) Ltd., Enterprise House, Wistaston Road Business Centre,
Wistaston Road, Crewe, Cheshire cw2 7rp United Kingdom
phone 01270 251 396 (local rate 0845 230 9601)
facsimile 01270 254 983; orders.uk@trafford.com
Order online at:
trafford.com/05-0291

10 9 8 7 6 5 4 3 2

Content

1   The More Within   2
2   Leaping Toadstools   7
3   A Canadian Kid's War   19
4   The Garden and the Golf Course   25
5   The Three and the Trees   29
6   Trees Like People   32
7   The Lake   46
8   The Foreboding Visitor   52
9   Chosen Goslings   54
10   Lone Wild Goose   70
11   Ducks and Others   74
12   The Bird at the Window   79
13   Best Friends, Kind Of   80
14   The Other Creatures   88
15   It Can Go Either Way   95
16   The Canoe   97
17   Nature's Farm   117
18   The Abandoned Clothes   125
19   Ending It All   132
20   Self Care   137
21   The Lonely Listener   140
22   Talk About Happiness   148
23   The Boy and His Teacher   155
24   Hugs Are Miracles, Too   163
25   It's Worth it   168
26   One Bike, Two Bikes, More   171
27   Though We See Through a Glass Dimly   177
28   A Week's Worth of Words to Live By   190

    References Cited   198
    Bibliography   200
    Index   201

Acknowledgments

To Lesley Crassweller for editing and
Chapter 2 "Leaping Toadstools"

To Dora Marose for her farm stories.

To unknown sources quoted.

And to all God's good earth and all
that's here to share and care for.

Preface

Goose Island Park has the power to get a person thinking about a whole lot of things that really matter.

If one persists in circling the park's lake, not out of habit, nor out of an obsession, but because it's the way one connects with the powers of nature, that person may find the experience, over time, very revealing.

Each experience gained through the senses stimulates, not only the imagination, but much more.

Trips around the park bring about journeys into the mind, picking out thoughts, memories, ideas, and dreams. The power of a park can do that, if one is open to it.

You are invited to participate in one person's venture where he experiences this power of the park. His particular journey came about during frequent visits to Henderson Park Lake in Lethbridge, Alberta, Canada.

Perhaps you may find this can happen to you, in the park near you.

Ken Crassweller
Lethbridge, Alberta, 2005

Dedication

To Lesley whose sharing and support mean so much to me.

"To him who in the love of Nature holds
Communion with her visible forms,
she speaks a various language." [1]

1

The More Within

"Go forth under the open sky, and list to Nature's teachings." 2

    A park can really do something to you. It can get you thinking, not only about what you see and hear, but about experiences you have had, memories, and even ideas that have lain dormant, buried deep within your mind. Take Henderson Park Lake, for example. It's not only a place to gain a sense of serenity, but it's a place to gain sensations that bring thoughts to mind, ones that offer "Aha!" moments. It's as though the park can talk, tell us things we never thought much about - and reconnect the neuron strings in our heads in new and different ways.

"Like many parks anywhere, 'Henderson Park' is a blend of relaxed leisure and active opportunities around a man-made lake. Paved and shale-bordered, Henderson Lake, once a large slough, includes playgrounds, rest areas, and picnic sites." Thus it is written in a tourist blurb, and rightly so!

But there is more. There are the you and me's, the many, including the creatures of water, land, and air that descend upon that otherwise "ho hum" mundane place, transforming it into something special. Why? Because nature's stirrings provide the music, and our personal experiences and observations provide the lyrics.

So, let's see if that is so, by getting us into the park by first searching for an entrance. We'll leave behind what borders the park, the paved artery, stop-and-go lights, anxious tailgaters, hotel signs, the sight of opulent homes with manicured lawns, the barren waste of the neighbouring exhibition grounds awaiting the invasion of the candyfloss midway - all of nature's unwelcomed house guests.

Hear lapping of water, wind through the trees, the wail of a distant train whistle, the Nikka Yuko Garden gong, the tap of a golf club hitting a ball, a mother goose calling straying goslings, and the squawk of a Blue Jay, playing children's laughter, shouting teens, and the swish of inline skates blend, giving the park a voice.
That voice is enhanced and embodied in the sights accentuated at the beginning and ending of each day when shadows define the shapes and forms of all that eyes can see. Neither harsh winds, clammy dampness, nor rudeness of sloppy rain, nor sleet, nor snow can rob this park, nor any park, of its beauty.

Not even the invading heavy odour of an oil seed plant, nor seasonal rotting stink of water weeds, nor aftershave and perfume smells on passers in the park, can steal away the park's attractions.

True, some days, attractions do become distractions, but only for a while. The brick and shale-paved paths suffer cuts and bruises like the walkers and runners who, too, suffer wear and tear. Brittle branches torn from trees by nasty winds and the odd maintenance contraption, slow down path users.

Sometimes a detour can become a pleasant habit walking over grass on the expansive lawns. An early walker in the dark may even be startled by the glaring lights of a worker's truck on the path. Despite the intrusions, little and big examples of sheer determination greet the eye with wonder. The little flowers poking their heads up through cracks in the path, a lone spindly tree clawing for a foothold among rocks lining the lake, and the thousands of interlocking pavement bricks, placed with care, forming the long path leading to the Japanese garden, attest to that. Such could humble even the most carefree park user who stopped to ponder.

"A perfect summer day is when the sun is shining, the breeze is blowing, the birds are singing, and the lawn mower is broken." [3]

Parks of all sizes and proportions, by their beauty and pristine state, at the outset cry out to be left alone. We creatures, like beavers, seem to demonstrate a need to satisfy our own desire for creature comforts. Sometimes it's overdone - not so in Henderson Park. Nature's integrity and human needs appear to have been achieved. Still, one can enjoy the lawns and lounging areas, the rose garden, children's playgrounds, group picnic shelters, concession booths, horse shoe pitch and group picnic shelter, washrooms, and lights along paths, informative sign-age, and even signs on washrooms alerting of surveillance cameras present, all without the plague of litter, or obtrusive policing.

Why this is all possible is to a great extent because of the war dead, whose names in remembrance are inscribed in bronze on stone cairns. Two other reminders layered with heavy grey paint point their First World War gun barrels across the water toward the Japanese garden, leaving any thoughtful person, lingering near them, with a sense of uneasy discomfort. Across the water, a symbol of peace and tranquility; nearby, symbols of war and violence. Thoughts evoked by those symbols of the present and the past are joined by symbols of hope for the future -the flags of Canada, Alberta, and the United Nations flap vigorously in the wind as statements of unity in diversity, and Canada's peacekeeping role.

Yet, some things are still missing.

Though the park had its beginning in 1912 for the 7th International Dry-Farming Congress, there isn't one plowshare on display. Nor are there any symbols commemorating what children who grew up during the wars went through.

Two frequent visitors to the park eyed the guns, then let their thoughts drift back to an earlier time where, for many, childhood was severely bruised by grown-up behaviour.

What did these guns evoke for others like them?

2

Leaping Toadstools
(A Child's War Memories)

The ack-ack guns on the sea front boomed again, reminding me of September 3rd, 1939 as a bunch of us kids walked home from school.

"Hey you kids know what? This afternoon at 3 o'clock a whistle will blow, and then the sirens, and then the bombs will start to drop on us!"

My stomach lurched as I looked at our little know-it-all friend, scurrying along with my twin brother, Keith, and me.

I knew there was a war coming, but not so soon - not like this. My brother grinned at me, and I knew I had more time. It was September, 1939.

The first siren came while I was leaning against the tall pole on which it was fastened, trying to tighten the foot clamp on my roller skates. With the first wail of the beast, I broke the record for an 8 -year-old scampering home to safety, but not without first falling over.

Reassured that it was only a test, my brother and I took to the outdoors, as we usually did, scanning the skies for aircraft, while hoping to not see any.

For six years we lived an anecdotal kind of life, filled with snippets of conversation gleaned from eavesdropping on the many adults of our extended family. Living in the southeast corner of England, we were to have a first hand encounter of a fairly horrible kind.

Gas masks - how we loathed them! I was always afraid there was gas lurking in the mask, and it would come out if I breathed too deeply. We carried them everywhere - to school and Sunday School, and on our general running around routes. They were housed in square cardboard boxes which quickly became makeshift footballs, often with the masks inside.

Sometimes when we sat in our school air raid shelter, the principal would order us to "don masks." I desperately tried to cheat by sticking my finger in the side of my mask so that I could breathe "real air." I usually got caught in the act as the teachers came to make sure the masks had a snug fit.

The school shelters were fun at first, as we raced in orderly lines from the school and down the shelter steps, to fling ourselves onto the hard benches. Teachers handed out milk and cookies if we were there long enough. But they soon got around to ordering us to take our books with us as we ran. We stalled, bringing books but forgetting paper or pencils. The lights were very dim and so we were within our rights clammering, "Please sir, we can't see the words."

Then we would sing. And that was great as we tried to drown out the sound of planes and gunfire.

Usually after the sirens sounded "All Clear" we were allowed to run home.

Keith and I would usually loiter along, eagerly searching the sky for airplane dog fights until an air raid warden shooed us off with, "You kids run along home, you shouldn't be out here."

We made plans to fight the enemy.

Keith knew how to make Molotov cocktails, he said. We planned to make some, climb a tree at the end of our street and hurl the bombs at any approaching enemy.

Never mind that we couldn't buy petrol, or had no empty bottles with which to make the bombs. Nor the fact, as Keith succinctly put it, "You know, if we see enemy soldiers, we won't climb trees, we'll run like h..."
He was about 9 years old by then and full of wisdom, not like his impetuous sister, who would jump first and look afterwards!

Dunkirk and Evacuations:

Uncle Charlie was a hero. He was a soldier, and he was also married to our Mum's youngest sister, Auntie Min. They lived across the road from us, in my grandparents' house.

Uncle Charlie was sent overseas early in the war. Keith and I heard lots of anxious talk, by eavesdropping around the aunts and uncles over at Gran's house. Finally the news of Dunkirk was on the radios and in the newspapers - and Uncle Charlie came home, rescued by some brave soul.

Skulking around we picked up snippets of Uncle Charlie's exploits. The one that fascinated me had me running off to our corner grocery and regaling the owner with: My Uncle Charlie and some other soldiers were actually rounding up prisoners when the order to retreat and evacuate came through. What to do with the prisoners?

One of Uncle Charlie's sidekicks turned on his prisoner with his bayonet fixed, said Charlie, "he begged for mercy but my pal said, Mercy you b..? I'll give you mercy," and he bayoneted the prisoner.

The store owner must have blanched at this filth coming from the lips of a nine-year-old, although the only comment I can remember him making was "Oh really?" Anyway, my obvious eavesdropping was severely curtailed, making me realize my tale- bearing had been brought to my elders' attention.

Uncle Charlie was later sent off to Italy, where he was wounded and kept as a prisoner in an Italian hospital, before being shipped off to a POW camp.

He wasn't the only one in our family to be evacuated from any place. As the pace of the war increased, the government ordered the evacuation of children from coastal areas.

Some families sent their children off to North America and didn't see them again until the war ended in 1945.

Our Mum and the "Aunts" conferred, and decided their kids would not go overseas, only inland.

So there we were one day, trudging off to the railway station with our gas masks, name tags on our lapels, and a bag lunch. Our school teachers and principal were with us.

All the Mums were crying, which didn't help too much. My mother's last instruction was to my brother, "You make sure you two stay together!"

I remember it being a long trip. The teachers didn't say much to us; they didn't even stop us eating our lunches too early. I remember watching one teacher slowly eating a great big bag full of gooseberries. She didn't give one to any of us. I kind of hoped she'd get a stomach ache!

When we reached our destination we were taken to a big hall with long tables and fed by a bunch of volunteer women. Then we were put into groups led by more volunteers with lists of names and addresses.

My sister and cousin, who were four years older than Keith and me, went off with one group. Keith and I were put in a group of about 7 or 8 kids and off we went with the list holder, trudging up and down the streets.

The people on the lists had evidently offered to take 1 or 2 evacuees, and we were now being delivered one kid here, 2 more there. Keith clutched my hand as though Mum's eyes were on him. Problems arose when we reached one house. The lady who came to the door looked us over and said, "I'll take the boy." Keith's hand tightened as he said, for the first of several times, "My Mum said we have to stay together." After considerable bickering, the lady finally relented and said she'd "take two instead of one."

I didn't like her and she didn't like me, so we were soon even. They had two teen-age girls, so welcomed having Keith around. I don't think the girls liked me too much, either. They were probably afraid they would have to babysit me or something.

We shared a school with the local kids, which meant we

only went to school half days. Things brightened up when all the mums were allowed to visit and all the kids got to show them off to the people boarding us.

Finally when the bombing on the coast and London got worse, most of the women were evacuated inland, so we got to see more of our Mums. In a short time, our Mum and the aunties got together and decided Hitler wasn't going to chase us out of our homes. So en masse we charged back to our home in Seaford. So many women reclaimed their kids and homes that the 'authorities' couldn't stop them.

Shortly after we returned, we learned of the 'terror of the night.' Dimly awake, only aware of my father's outstretched arms, and hearing nothing but a mad, wailing shriek that has never fully left my mind, I leapt upwards to be caught in those arms and hustled to the air raid shelter. In the morning our terror was somewhat relieved when we discovered that our school had been bombed. Our fun didn't last long, as arrangements were made for us to have classes in the senior school.

Another air raid I recall easily, happened before the air raid siren was sounded. We were sitting near our fireplace when suddenly there was a huge whoomph, and then a sort of blankness. Then I realized I was on my hands and knees in the corner of the room, and all the lights were out. Mum was hollering because the windows were broken. I don't remember where Keith was. In fact I don't remember how or when I was blown out of my chair. I just was!

One of the highlights of the war was when Canadian soldiers occupied the buildings of a "private" girls school in our little town. The students and the staff had been evacuated inland.

Keith and I and our friends played happily in the school

fields and chatted with some of the soldiers. One told us he was an "Indian" and his name was Archie. We were pretty impressed at having spoken to a real Indian!

When the grass was finally cut, we would push the "hay" into the shapes of Spitfires or tanks and invent great war maneuvers. I think the soldiers were pretty amused - one told my dad that "the girl is a real sergeant major."

We also found that several of the vacated private schools had left their orchards unattended. That begged for 'scrumping raids' for apples and pears. On the odd occasion when an old gardener did show up in the middle of a raid, we would flee away, laughing and shouting. One time we leapt over a low stone wall, only to find that the drop was considerably deeper on the other side.

British soldiers also played a part in our lives. One day they came trudging through the town on a long march, stopping for a rest in the grass near the end of the street. We ran home to get water and lemonade for them. They'd probably have preferred something else, but that's what our mother sent in two big jugs.

On another occasion, while we were prying around where we shouldn't have been, a soldier asked us if we had seen a bunch of soldiers near by. We hadn't, but decided to go looking for them. As we peeped over a small embankment, we were horrified to see a whole army racing toward us over a nearby field. Those rifles looked as though they were pointed right at us - we turned and fled in terror, even though we knew they were "our guys."

There was a funny side to the war. Somewhere along the way, a country that had been "the enemy" now became a "gallant friend" and Clementine Churchill established an Aid to Russia fund. So we kids got together and had an outdoor concert and 'jumble sale,' sending the resulting money off to Mrs. Churchill. I remember we got a letter back, thanking us for "helping the gallant Russians in the glorious defense of their country."

Those words sprang back to mind a few years later when England and Russia were again at loggerheads during the Cold War.

Another weird episode occurred when we were living in a tiny village in the midlands. My mother was a cook at a private school which had been evacuated from the coast, while my Dad was in Coventry.

Anyway, without either Keith or me hearing it, a German plane crashed at night by a little stream near the school. It was believed the pilot fell into the water and drowned.

When we got up, the place was swarming with soldiers who set up a guard over what was left of the plane. I can't remember if they stayed in huts on the grounds or had tents. But I remember that in what had been the stables they set up a huge wooden frame on which they wove camouflage nets, and even let me weave in a few bits of green and khaki stuff.

The soldiers spent a lot of time carving things from the plane's perspex windows. One of them made an ornament to give to the school's headmistress when they left.

Sometime during the early years of the war, we were all issued with identification tags. They were made of a compressed cardboard, and imprinted with our identity number.

We quickly learned them. Mine was EJNI 2904. My brother, who was born 20 minutes after me, was one rung down the ladder, so his was EJNI 2905. We were quite proud of them - we were supposed to wear them all the time. But then we found out WHY we were wearing them -

As a school friend said, "Didn't you know that? It's for knowing who you are if you get dug out from a bombed house." Somehow the discs lost their charm.

Our dad was transferred to Coventry with the Civil Defense. It was after the big bombing which destroyed a lot of the city.

We were housed in a flat (apartment) which had suffered bomb damage. I remember leaning on the fire place mantel, only to have it give way and getting a cut on my hand.

Although we had few air raids, we were scared out of our wits one night shortly after the siren had sounded. The air was filled with a sound like immense gunfire and swooshes, unlike the normal anti aircraft noises. My Dad rushed outside with his helmet on. The rest of us ran to crouch in the hallway, with my brave mother standing over us with her arms outspread.

Finally the noise stopped and Dad came back in with a big grin - a new type of rocket gun had been installed along with the ack-ack guns. The racket came from the rockets which burst into boxlike formation around enemy planes. So we breathed again.

Another time, closer to the end of the war, we were back visiting in Seaford. Our cousin Derek, a few years older than us, asked if we had seen the new German V1 and V2 buzz bombs. We hadn't.

Again, a siren went. We hung out the bedroom window. "Here comes one," Derek shouted, and we heard what sounded like an airborne motor bike. We watched, literally rooted in excited fear. A long cigar-shaped object with small fins at the back, came into view. There was a red light glowing at the back.

Suddenly, the light went out. "What do we do now?" we asked Derek.

He was halfway along the hall leading to the stairs. "Run like hell," he shouted, and we did - to the backyard shelter. The bomb exploded more or less harmlessly, in mid air. They did real damage when they landed and exploded!

We did have some fun during the war. I remember being in one little village when a new friend invited me to go to Brownies. Not having been a Brownie, I was fascinated by a huge "toadstool" which was used in their ceremonies. One night I couldn't resist - I just had to leap over that toadstool!

Brown Owl was not amused and suggested that perhaps I shouldn't be there if I couldn't stop leaping toadstools. So I left.

Keith fared better in Coventry where he joined the Air Scouts, a new branch of the Boy Scouts.

Later, in Brighton, I joined the Girls Guildry. We had a neat uniform and an interesting program. I remember we attended a Thanksgiving service at the end of the war, marching in our uniforms in a parade with other young people as well as the military units. A retired captain who lived on our street would always salute me when he saw me in uniform. It felt good.

One of the biggest banes of "my war" was the air raid shelter.

At first we all had little Anderson shelters, usually in the back yard, and a very miserable place to be. I believe they were sunk into the ground a bit then completely covered with piles of dirt. They were cold and usually damp and didn't feel in the least secure.

Sometimes we would run into the cupboard under the staircase. We even put chairs in there. At least we didn't have to run outside, and it was warm.

The shelter I really dreaded was the Morrison shelter. It was located in our sitting room - a huge thing like a big steel table. I remember we had mattresses on the floor part, and also on the top, so we could sleep if the air raid went on that long.

The shelter was constructed in such a way that, once everyone was inside, more or less lying down, long grids were pulled across the open side, presumably to keep out debris if the house should collapse.

Our family of five grew to seven when my eldest sister, married to a young Canadian airman who became a prisoner of war, came home with their baby. Togetherness in the shelter was a thing of claustrophobic horror.

One night the siren went. My aunt and uncle, plus a young cousin, were visiting us. Into the shelter we all went, laid out like cordwood. My Dad and my uncle stayed outside, thrusting their heads under when the guns were going off.

I was just thankful that they couldn't put the grid into place and close us in.

We often went off to school the next day wearing the clothes we had slept in. We were a crumpled looking lot - but then, so were we all!

My brother and I often recall events of the War, which occupied most of our growing-up years. We laugh a lot but we also remember the fears and the sounds.

We were 8 years old by September, 1939, lighthearted, athletic youngsters who had no doubts that we would have a future. How fortunate we were in that respect. But how much did we lose, along with all those other thousands of youngsters who lived through the war in Great Britain?

Perhaps our biggest loss was the chance to know a carefree childhood, which of course, we could never regain. War takes something from everyone.

We were little kids in 1939. In May, 1945, we went to a great outdoor celebration with my father in Brighton, where we were living. We were 13 years old. The war was over.

In July we turned 14, left school and went to work. We were adults.

3

A Canadian Kid's War

"Who live under the shadow of war,
What can I do that matters? " 4

When I was a kid, I wondered what I could do when my dad and brother were away. The answer came. I'd take a few cents each week to school. My teacher had a big picture of a soldier in his underwear. He needed dressing. Each bit of money that we, as a class, came up with, would buy a piece of his uniform or "kit." Still we never bought him a gun. We also brought money to pay for a Red Cross membership card and a small tin badge with a red cross on it. We would wear it at meetings, usually Friday afternoon when we weren't watching National Film Board black and white movies in the auditorium.

I wasn't happy when my dad was away in the army. I never heard from him and didn't get to read his letters to

Mom. During those years my brother, who served in the Governor General Horse Guards, was but a faint memory. My memory was jogged only when I thumbed through the family photo albums and saw pictures of him in shorts, standing in front of a barracks door that had a light above his head. In a couple of pictures he was holding a gun and had a gas mask covering his face. I got a bit of a clearer picture of who he was, seeing the photo of him standing proudly at ease with my dad, and granddad, two in khaki brown, and Grandpa, "old Bill," in Legion tam and tie.

Just as I had tried to get closer to my dad by poking around in his stuff at home, I tried to get closer to my brother by doing the same. I wore his skull cap made by turning a fedora inside out and serrating the edges, and coveted his Boy Scout first class hat badge, scout hat, and other stuff. It wasn't till after the war that I heard from my sister-in-law that he felt there was nothing to come home to. All his stuff was gone. When I got older, I felt bad about that.

After the war, I had wondered as a kid why he didn't want to go with my dad to kill ducks and other birds. It didn't occur to me that he had seen enough killing. He never shared his feelings about the war with many of us in the family.

Somehow permission was never given to share or take seriously feelings of family members. So his feelings of loss stayed buried for sometime. His wife, told me about some of his traumatic moments, such as the time when he and an army buddy stopped their lorries at a bridge to discuss the odds of hitting a land mine, possibly planted either on the bridge or in the water. He chose the bridge, the most likely mined bit, according to his friend, who chose to cross the stream. He lived. His friend got blown to pieces. Like my dad, who said little about WW1, he never shared the pain with me that he carried from WW2, other than to say one thing that I'll not forget. Once near his death, he said this about the war:

"We were kids. We got so that we didn't really care about tomorrow. We loved and lived for the day."

When I thought back to what my brother must have gone through, I'd had it really easy. As a kid of just 17, in battle he faced fear daily. The biggest thing I ever had to face as a kid was keeping my nose clean (keeping out of trouble) at school, and avoiding the gangs hanging around at Chees's café on Fifth Avenue. They were some of the guys who kicked my bike spokes in while I visited the library.

I remember at night when I was eight or nine and my brother was overseas fighting, I'd go to bed with my Dagwood double and triple deck sandwiches of onions, tomatoes, and stuff and I'd pray "Kill all the Nazis." I wanted my dad and brother home with me!

To do my part, I also cut out Life Magazine pictures of army tanks, planes, guns, lots of war stuff, and pasted them in scrap books to show battle scenes.

Thinking back to the nineteen forties, I wonder how my dad felt about war. He didn't, on the surface, seem to have any second thoughts back then of joining up to become a corporal in the Veteran Guards. Despite his horrible WW1 experiences he insisted in getting back into uniform. He was too old for overseas but that didn't stop him. He put his maroon Mercury car up on blocks and went away. He ended up guarding German prisoners of war with his friends. My dad had lots of friends. I often wondered how many were German prisoners. I also wondered whether his bosses picked him to guard Germans because they thought he had a German last name. Once when my dad was on leave he brought me, as a surprise, two models of German submarines and a Christopher Columbus-type sailing ship model.

    Many of those that he guarded were sub crews. Dad's gifts, made by crew members, were intricately made to scale. The submarine models, just like the real thing, had fins, rudders, propellers and more, that is until I floated them in the water at the beach and shot at them with my Beebee gun. What I didn't wreck soon disintegrated in the water. The glue gave way, and even the fine toothpick decks parted company, along with the conning tower details. It was too bad that I didn't value them. I just couldn't, feeling that those who made them kept me from my dad. I guess I was just jealous that the prisoners saw more of my dad than I and the family did, while waiting in Regina.

    When my dad was away, I would proudly show my friends his old ball glove. It was black, worn, frayed, and without a pocket. It hung ceremoniously on a nail in the veranda across from mom's geranium plants. I was also proud of the spurs from my dad's WW1 days. He was in the Horse Artillery back then. I found other treasures. Hidden among the cobwebs and rafters down stairs in our home were some 1920's spats, and in my dad's bedroom dresser, besides his railway man's watch, and two revolvers, were some medals from the First World War.

    My dad never spoke about seeing all the slaughter he saw in WW1, nor did my brother speak about what he saw. It must have been awful. I never did see my dad or brother enough during WW2 to listen in on what they had to say to each other about the fighting. Even when they were home I got the idea that it was a no-no to ask them about it. Yet, they did seem to pay some attention to me. Once both he and my brother got leave at the same time. Their willingness to help me finish building a model plane was great, at least at first. I was just putting the finishing touches on it after having struggled with balsa strips and paper. I was looking forward to flying it by winding its elastic band tightly by turning the prop many times. Before I got to fly it, dad and my brother decided that it needed a paint job. A can of grey house paint would do. It did, making it so heavy that the puny elastic band wouldn't power it off the ground. So there it sat on the shelf, a reminder of my dad's and brother's affection for me.

Better times ahead - Dad and my brother sat in the front room. Each in turn, at my asking, drew pictures of guns and other weapons that they used. I was thrilled. I remembered before my brother went to war, he had made some drawings of army tents with flags on them. But guns were even better! Maybe!

For years after WW2 I wanted to join the military so I could really feel like I was one with the three men, my granddad, dad, and brother, whose picture was taken by the guns at the Legislative buildings. I believed, no chance though, since I thought my feet were flat, and my eyes were crappy. Still, my prayers were answered later in life. I never did have flat feet and I could see with glasses. I still had an urge to join the army but I was too chicken to apply, believing I'd fail the physical with my eyes. Rejection would have been hard to take. Besides, by then I was starting to hunch that war was wrong because of what it did to people. My conviction became rock solid when I read in a newspaper about young kids in a town in Europe playing soccer using a human skull as a substitute for a ball.

As the years passed and buds of youth wilted and died, park donors' cairns and benches in memory of loved ones sprouted up to augment the park furnishings. Where easy chairs in homes remained briefly empty, reminders of loved ones who left through death, simple things like benches for tired bones in nature's living room, reminded one of life and the urging of nature's hospitality.

4

The Garden and the Golf Course

"The trees of the Lord are watered abundantly...
In them the birds build their nests. " 5

That's strange! No, it's not! That's neat! Now there's a mystery. Who did it? Who planted and nurtured those flowering plants hugging the golf course side of the fence, and why? The chain links with some angling overhang barbed wire, walls off the narrow path between the golf course and the Nikka Yuko Garden which, too, has a fence, but is free of barbed wire. In the Fall the flowers which took away the starkness of the fence die off, but coloured leaves, clinging to the chain links, take over the task. The human effort to beautify is bolstered by nature that never lets an honest effort down.

Hints of activity in motion, are golf balls striking the fence on one side of the path, and fluttering bird wings on the other. Moving down the narrow path between those two contrasting approaches to commune with nature, one can stop, ponder, and compare and contrast each with the other. The park offers that opportunity, a chance also to see and experience two distinctly different world views expressed in the design of each, the golf course, and the garden.

Like most Japanese gardens, Nikka Yuko garden brings life to the ordinary with the extraordinary, "using trees, shrubs, rocks, pebbled beaches, ponds, stone lanterns, granite basins, rain-catching stones, moss to create rich background textures, aged bonsai trees, all to provide visual beauty and hidden meanings." The included bridges offer ways to cross, pause and "enjoy the small things in life that are so easily and quickly overlooked in our fast paced world."

Where the designed vastness of green, sprinkled with trees, sand, mounds, waters in streams and ponds of the golf course, despite its beauty, challenges and frustrates; the garden in its passive peacefulness allows visitors to calm their souls; to approach life relaxed, rather than attack it aggressively.

True, by a Japanese garden there could be found "a Sentinel stone used to symbolize warriors, deities, and fictional heroes: but, it's usually found at the garden's entrance gate, perhaps to indicate what will be left behind after one enters the garden." It is true that such is also often found near the entrance of a golf course. There the warriors metal armour are the vehicles in the parking lot, and the warriors are in the club house, rather than in the garden's tea house.

The Nikka Yuko Garden, rich in texture and symbolism is a "Stroll Garden." Such gardens have hills to represent mountains, streams and miniature lakes, waterfalls, rocky islands occupying off centred positions in the lakes with some low junipers or picturesque pines.

Unlike golf courses, it's been said these gardens are the essence of nature, representing a beauty that is quiet and refined, a consistent beauty that changes through the seasons. There is found:

"A quiet beauty that reflects the perfect balance found in nature" 6

There is found an "Illusion of space and distance... to capture the feelings of peace in heart and soul" 7

Compare that with what one author said about golf:

"We learn so many things from golf - how to suffer, for instance." 8

Whereas in the garden, "An expanse of natural scenery... the visitor is invited to be still, meditate and contemplate the wonder of creation."

On the golf course there is an invitation to "... spent a day in a round of strenuous idleness." 9

One author contradicted a common view of golf. "They say golf is like life, but don't believe them. Golf is more complicated than that." 10

Contrast that with the stream of quiet thought inherent in the garden that can lead, for some, to a very uncomplicated life in tune with nature: the way of attaining Buddhahood adhering to the "Six Paramita: Giving, Discipline, Patience, Endeavor (effort), Meditation, Wisdom."

Whatever lasting impression, and/or direction to which the Nikka Yuko Garden leads the visitors , it does have "the ability to bring a person back to their sense of 'self' in our hurried, industrialized world."

5

The Three and the Trees

Three piners ambled down the path throwing words at each other as they looked around at what was growing and moving. The first said,

"See all them living things. We should let them go to it, go at each other. Let the fittest, the strongest win out, like in nature there."

The second said, "No way. You can't just let them all run wild. What about the weakest link in the human chain? You got to take care of them, use some basic principles, set them up as rules, and enforce them, like rules in a game. Then all will work out okay. "

The third piped in. "Both of you are wrong. You've got to step in, control and regulate what's happening. It's not a jungle out there. We've got to make it so the most good happens for the most people. You just can't have a few get the most of the riches, and the rest get the crumbs. That wouldn't be fair. Sure in nature, the runts in the litter get short shrift, and die. But this Darwinism stuff about the strongest survive? Strengthening the gene bank is fine for animals, but we ain't animals."

The three walked on, so caught up in their own arguments that they appeared oblivious to others passing on the path. Often some passers-by, aghast at the three's carelessness, bundled their children into their arms, and stepped off the path to avoid harm from the three hogging the path.

After much argumentative hullabaloo, the three eventually searched for some common ground.
"Trees, that's the ticket! Let's talk about trees," one said.
" Right, let's do that," the second agreed.
The third scoffed, " Say what? You got to be kidding. You can't be serious!"
"Sure can! Trees got a lot to say about people, and people about trees."
"That's right," said the second. "Both trees and humans, they're much alike, both have limbs, and stuff flowing through them. Think about it - lots in common, even more. "
" Exactly, where are you two going with this anyway?"
"What?"
"Trees and humans."
"You figure it out."
"I will."
"Me too."
"Then what? "
"Up to you."
"Well," said the second, "since we got all caught up in this tree business, I've consulted the oracle."

"The what?"

"You know, that little book I always have stuffed in my back pocket, the one that you thought was a bird watcher book?"

"Oh, yes. At first I thought you were a real brain."

"Well, anyway, here is some stuff about trees. Thought you two would be interested in these quotes from my 'know it all book.' Do you want to hear, and be enlightened?"

"Okay, if you must."

" Plants are the young of the world, vessels of health and vigor; but they grope ever upward toward consciousness; the trees are imperfect men, and seem to bemoan their imprisonment, rooted in the ground." 11

"A few minutes ago every tree was excited, bowing to the roaring storm, waving, swirling, tossing their branches in glorious enthusiasm like worship. But though to the outer ear these trees are now silent, their songs never cease." 12

" You can't be suspicious of a tree, or accuse a bird or a squirrel of subversion or challenge the ideology of a violet."
13

"I never saw a discontented tree. They grip the ground as though they liked it, and though fast rooted they travel about as far as we do." 14

"So, what do you think about all that. Good eh?"

"I suppose," said one.

"Sounds pretty highfalutin to me!" said the other.

6

Trees Like People

Eventually, the three piners did settle on playing a game of comparing trees to people, in particular politicians and other public figures. They began tree spotting - maybe figuring that one can say more about what trees have in common with people, than what birds have.

So on they walked, taking turn about, using their own common idioms to describe the characteristics of different trees they could match up with people.

"Wow!" gasped one of the piners "Look at that tree over there - it's as beautiful as the day is long. It kind of says, life is a bowl of cherries. The only thing is, it seems it's all dressed up and nowhere to go. It appears to know what's up, and casts a long shadow. It is tried and true, above board, one that a creature could put its hopes on, and get the red carpet treatment from. Now that's a tree for all seasons. Just like one or more politicians that I know, someone you can really count on."

"Now, let's not get carried away," said the second, who looked further down the path,

"Take a gander at that one. Now, there's one ancient tree! Long in the tooth, with a scarred wind- worn face, it seems over the hill. Still, it's an oldie and a goodie. Deep-rooted with its feet firmly planted in the ground floor, it obviously had a good beginning which will make a good ending.

"Now, its neighbour, on the other hand, across the way, seems so straight-laced, a bit of a wet blanket with a heart of stone. If it could, it would, no doubt, throw cold water on anyone trying to improve the path. A few feet away, there is another neighbour, the most unimaginative type, one who just hunkers down, and seems to think it's got all bases covered. Resting on its laurels, it looks like its just marking time, despite that times, they are a-changing."

The third piner, exclaimed, "Yep, times are a-changing. So also do trees like people - change for sure. You can see that in the tree just ahead, the one with the middle-age spread. It appears to be busting a gut. Things just aren't what they used to be for it, for sure! For what you see is what you get. Though, maybe that holds true from the beginning. You just can't make a silk purse out of a sow's ear. Just look. "The handwriting is on the wall. It's shedding bark, and going bald, and demanding a lot of attention from park caretakers. That just goes to show that the more things change, the more things stay the same-same old, same old!"

The first piner, rather than comment about his two friends' views, pointed to some saplings, saying, "Chips off the old block - planted between the path and the lake, with the thinking that the old timers will kick the bucket, and sooner or later need replacing. Look, they are lithe and lean, adolescents, wet behind the ears; knee high to grasshoppers, and growing like weeds, the pick of the litter, yet still mere babes in the woods.

"Ah, to be young and foolish trees, new kids on the block who find humans eager to give them a hand, or at least offer them props and ties to hold them up, to help them stand against winds of change till, firmly rooted, their backbones grow strong.

Just look at those restless saplings, quivering in the wind, like they've got ants in their pants. You'd think there is no time like the present to seek greener pastures, for their autumn immature seeds. They haven't heard yet that rolling stones gather no moss, and that good things come to those who wait, and that it's a game of inches."

Having heard all that attention given to youth, the third piner gave his friend a nudge and pointed out that there were a great number of old weathered trees that had been around the block and, having been young once, could say, 'Been there, done that.' Those weathered trees, and their impressive presence throughout the park, presented a stark contrast to those saplings who needed to cure their enthusiasm. As youngsters, "they just had too much sail for their small craft."

The second piner, impressed with such expounded wisdom added, "If one of those old weathered trees could talk they might give this advice to those persnickety saplings.

'No sense going overboard to keep up with the Jones. As saplings, wet behind the ears, you've tried winging it time after time with no success. You need to take a step back, take stock, and realize that what you are trying to make happen isn't all it's cracked up to be. You, as saplings, have a long row to hoe, and miles to go before you sleep. You've got to crawl before you can walk. Let the dust settle, and let the future raise the bar a few notches, so that you can become the best that you can be."

The other two piners looked at their friend who had expounded so lucidly. One then expounded with equal veracity. He spoke about the saplings, describing what he thought was their impending downfall as trees that hadn't a clue that they were trees. Despite the improbable pictures his choice of words conveyed, he trucked on, giving no thought of whether what he said made any sense, in so far as to what trees are capable of achieving.

"But the ambitious saplings looked like they were ready to go, thinking, no time like the present to go for broke! It appeared that, especially for some, having come from the wrong side of the tracks, they wanted to have a leg up. They wanted a place in the sun. They had high hopes, and wanted to rise up so that they could look beyond as far as the eye could see, to take the world by storm, and in quick time, go out in a blaze of glory. Could they hear some nearby say that those saplings are just too big for their breeches? They are already over their heads. What a tangled web they weave, thinking everything is up for grabs. They forget that altitude is determined by attitude - and they shouldn't be too hasty, for what goes up must come down."

Some other park tree residents, more impressive, a little bigger, and by the looks of them, a little wiser, though still diamonds in the rough, chose the path less traveled, and seemed to be on the cutting edge of what is, and what could be; and were, without a doubt, more creative. What they were doing shouted out, "You ain't seen nothing yet!" For the ends of their limbs looked like they were working their fingers to the bone, busy as bees making seeds, from the crack of dawn, until the cows came home, all in a day's work. No question about it, they were gluttons for punishment.

Nearby, and scattered through the park, a bunch of trees didn't follow suit. They were running wild, walking on the wild side, fit to be tied, making whoopee, and as some trees go, having the time of their lives.

A few regulars on the park path shared how they thought some other trees, legends in their own minds, were getting off on the wrong foot. Mouthy, all talk and no action, they were biting off more than they could chew, keeping company in their branches with nasty, noisy birds, whose droppings had their tree hosts paint themselves into a corner, forgetting that what goes down, comes around, ending with someone eating crow.

Some did eat crow. Others still were pushy, getting the first piner's goat. In frustration, he shouted out, "Why on God's green earth do some trees have to act like bulls in a china shop."
To that, another piner sanctimoniously replied, "Well, you gotta break a few eggs to make an omelette." Whereon the third said, " But that doesn't cut it. The pushy ones are all over the map, just going too far, taking it to the limit. By the look of it, a few of the muscular, heavy-limbed appeared out to exert their macho-masculinity by kicking some butt. They were making no bones about it."

Just then, after the third piner had given his two cents worth, a wrinkle-browed runner on the path stopped dead in her tracks as she was about to pass the three piners trudging along with their mouths full of words. She looked like she was going to give breathing room to the passers-by trying to get around the self-absorbed piners who were all arms and elbows. If trees could talk, they might say, "It was obvious the considerate runner was after the piners' Achilles' heels to help them turn over a new leaf."

The piners paid no heed to that runner, or for that matter to any others on the path, for they were on a mission, intent on portraying the personalities of the trees that they felt so resembled the personalities of human species.

One began to wonder, though, if each of the three piners was unconsciously picking out trees to talk about, that closely resembled personality traits in him, or on the hand, portrayed traits that the choosers didn't like about themselves.

One of the three, the most rambunctious of the lot, got all het up about one particular tree that got his attention by the park's pier. "Just look at that one. Now there is a bully if ever there was one, a real threat to its neighbours. Somehow its presence just causes one to get tensed up, just looking at it, just waiting for the other shoe to drop. You just would never know when it would drop a heavy piece of itself on your head, or let the wind tear one of its limbs off and hurl it in your direction. A mean sucker, that one is! "

"Well, at least you know where you stand with that one," said another of the three piners. Some other trees, you never know whether they're bluffing or not. At least you know you've got to handle that one with kid gloves. But what do you do with the ones that, especially in a storm, sway, creak, and make a big production of themselves, waving their limbs at you in a threatening way?

"How do you approach them when you find that their specie's bark is bigger than their bite, that their bluffs are all bark? A mite bit embarrassing, don't you think, when you find that, by taking them seriously, you are seen as barking up the wrong tree. For such trees are no threat at all, and, if the truth be told, couldn't fight their way out of wet paper bags.

"One might even find, as with some people, though their threatening demeanor suggests they've ice in their veins, and don't even give a hoot, that they do care, are sensitive - and are really using their up-front gruffness to cover up a weak sense of self."

The third piner, having heard all that sympathizing stuff

about some poor messed up trees, like some people he knew, said, "That's a lot of claptrap. There oughta be a law against people getting sucked into feelin sorry for bullies and the likes. They've got nerve thinking their trouble is only the lack of understanding from others. They're a real pain in the neck. All they do is make my blood boil! "

The piner shuffling along beside him turned and said, "Look, don't get carried away, you'll burst a blood vessel."
"Well, you know what I mean!"
"Sure, but those types are few and far between. Take a look at that bunch of trees over there. They're a far cry from blood boilers. See. They're healthy, opened branched, limbs in motion, very much alive. They picture for me healthy specimens that could, if not so rooted, be hard at it in a competitive sports as team-players in winning combinations, jockeying for position, exuding vibrant healthiness. As luck would have it, when push comes to shove, nature's down-siders, like those blood-boilers you growled about, just can't hold a candle to those trees that are like competitor performers who can, with effort, win hands down. "

The three piners kept up their stop and go progress around the lake, peering about, and like bird watchers, now and then, enthused by their finds, sharing their observations, and opinions with vigour and conviction.

"Say, look at that pathetic sight over there," one said to the others. " Did you ever see such a nervous, anxious and cautious, unsure of itself- looking thing? Now, there is a real basket case of a tree. It looks like it will never stand up and be counted. Gosh, it's on tenter hooks, wound tighter than a spring. If it were human, no doubt it would have butterflies in its stomach, waiting with baited breath for the next shoe to drop. If it were a person, I'd tell it that there is no rhyme nor reason why it couldn't at least test the waters and risk, not worry so much, and only cross the bridge when it comes to it, rather than stewing about things. That's the kind of tree, like a few people I've run across, that maybe isn't even capable of looking on the bright side. "

"So what do you do about them?"
"I don't know, give them a big hug maybe?"
"Hard to say."

"Just about as hard to say anything about that spooky, mystery tree near the pavilion there - so different from the one we've just talked about, " said the second piner. "That tree, like some persons, reveals little about its outlook, bright or gloomy. If it had been human, it would be one who played its cards close to its chest."

" Darn it, since you pointed that one out to us," said the first, "I too felt, in that one, there is more than meets the eye. In fact, I've not been able to make heads or tails of what that one's about. I'm one, as you know, who doesn't beat around the bush, but with that unknown quantity, I'd be barking up the wrong tree if I assumed that I knew what made that tree tick. Though, I do accept that it's what's inside that counts, but I just can't put my finger on it. Still, where there is smoke, there's fire, but darn it, I just can't locate the fire. I guess one just has to accept that, as with some people, it will remain a mystery."

Beyond those mystery trees, but still in the park, were some trees that appeared to be loners, misfits that caused piners to shrug, and accept - to each his own - and that you can't fit square pegs into round holes. So, if some break ranks with the crowd, and choose to distance themselves from others, maybe that's okay. Though, more than one piner thought, if only the loner could risk, moved by the idea that today is the first day of the rest of one's life.

Throughout the park, near the lake shore, and beyond, near the road bordering the park, some trees looked the worse for wear, unlike the mystery and loner ones. They revealed that they'd had a rough time, and somewhere along the way had missed the boat. Maybe they could have done better in their early growth years, but hindsight is 20/20. Still, at the end of the day, maybe things will go better for them. Who knows? That didn't convince one sceptic piner who peered around at those who didn't seem to stand a chance, and mumbled, "They're not out of the woods yet," and added, "I thank my lucky stars, I'm not one of them."

"You and me both," one of his fellow piners said. "It wouldn't be much fun feeling lonely, a forgotten one, who, out of sight, out of mind felt he'd fallen through the cracks, and got a raw deal living in the park. "
"Something like how the passed-by for promotions hard-working guys must feel, right?"
"Yes, something like that. Though I can't imagine a tree being ambitious. That seems to be reserved for the human race."
The last piner, having been only listening, piped up then, "The one you two have been referring to isn't the only one who could be thought to have gotten a raw deal. Look at that tree just ahead of us. It's leaning, bowing, and off-kilter, and needs to be propped up. It looks like it's had a really rough time. If a friend of mine looked that wounded, even my saying, 'keep your chin up,' wouldn't help. I'm afraid while trying to cheer him up, I'd be thinking, knock on wood; I'm not that way."

Other trees, too, were off-kilter, finding themselves caught up in other difficult predicaments. Through some twist of fate, they had zigged when they should have zagged, and as a result were all bent out of shape, looking hammered. Yet, though distorted and ugly to some, they were attractive to others.

The park, with all that it could offer wasn't able to help all to be the best that they could be. Some trees had bark that lost its lustre with acne and warts, all of which they needed like holes in the head. Others, cancerous, rotted from the inside out, down to their bare bones. Still, some skate boarders and in-line skaters who flew by them saw glimmers of hope in their clinging to life, despite the trauma they suffered.

Squeezed in among those, out of sight of the skaters, a few trapped trees, boxed in, looked as though they had their backs against the wall, between rocks and hard places. Regardless of whether, as they grew, they did or didn't reach out with their limbs - to push away those crowding them, their predicament reminded one piner, that, like them, there are folks who feel there is no use trying to stick their necks out and risk. Big Brother may be watching and if one does risk, there is a good chance he'd stomp down, and put one in his place.

"So," the piner said to another, "Some just knuckle under, give in, give up, pack it in, and refuse to risk or even go beyond square one. "

The piners' journey around the lake had got them to where they passed by the children's play area. Stopping to look a little closer at some trees along the path, they could see a tree that had suffered much abuse. It sure looked like it had got the stuffing knocked out of it, and had up to now lived a dog's life. There was evidence that it had been put down when it had tried to grow erect and proud. Its life appeared to be for the birds.
The squeal of wind whirling about in its bruised branches, caused the piners to imagine a desperate cry as an outburst of helpless rage. One of the piners said to the other two, "You know that brings to mind for me the battered women suffering domestic violence. I've heard the reception a few got when they left the violence and ran home to their moms

and dads. No doubt, each in anger, most likely swore vengeance, only to hear, 'Forget it. Two wrongs don't make a right, and besides, you've made your bed, now lie in it. But remember, time heals all wounds.' Not much comfort there, nor was there comfort in the words of a well- meaning neighbour friend of her parents who said, 'You may be surprised, the shoe may eventually be on the other foot, you may have the last laugh."

Often, in addition to the piners, some other walkers differed as they talked back and forth en route around the lake. One would say, "Look at that pathetic tree, wishy washy as all get out, making no effort to be useful, offer shade, or anything else. "
The other would reply, "You may think it's taking the line of least resistance, but remember, you can't judge another till you have walked in his shoes,"
The response? "That would be a trick!"

Passing judgment on some trees did seem to be, at times, a sport for some, other than the piners beating the well-worn paths.

It wasn't unusual to hear, "That's a clumsy one. The left hand doesn't know what its right hand is doing. It's even all thumbs. What a bump on the log. Really, as useless as a lead balloon, rough around the edges."

"Hmm ...."

Then there were others, not piners, nor critical passers by, but the commercially successful scurrying through the park with no time to waste- nor time to express impatience with a few unhappy campers - trees so bedraggled and out of sorts.

That is, all but one who was hurrying through the park,

looking neither left nor right. That one exception seemed vexed as he, meaning business, ran, throwing up his hands in frustration shouting over his shoulder. The piners that saw him fly by them, wondered whether he was annoyed with them, perfect strangers, or in his madness was shouting at the trees, "Oh, jump in the lake, surely you can see that there is no time but the present. What are you waiting for? What's stopping you? Has your get up and go, gone and went?"

Not all park visitors lacked understanding or empathy. One peered at a piner-targeted tree, and shouted, "Can't you see that tree is slowly dying? Time is running out for it. It's suffering death by a thousand cuts. What a way to go. Despite what you say or think its agenda is its own. Look. Its bags are all packed and ready to go. It's ready for the Last Hurrah. It's ready to be pushing up daisies, knowing that we're all here today, and gone tomorrow, and that history will continue repeating itself. We're all in the same boat you know. It comes to us all."

One could imagine why some other sad looking trees looked the way that they did. That is, as if they had nothing to drink. But, there were some whose limbs were as dry as bones, despite the fact that there was water, water everywhere.

The piners had talked about a lot of sad cases as some talk about family members, friends, people they meet on the street, and at work.

But not all was doom in gloom among the park's tree population. It appeared that many played the hands they were dealt. They demonstrated that it is better to light a candle than curse the darkness.
For them when things got tough, the tough got going. They seemed to see the living process as duck soup, and so they

passed with flying colours, and thrived in the park - inspirations to the humans passing through their home.

   Among those positive performers were some of their contemporaries who were sociable among themselves and with others. So open and inviting they were, so close, that many seemed even joined at the hips. Some piners commented, "Aha, we know where they're coming from, birds of a feather, flock together. "
   Despite being only trees, they showed by their swaying bodies and limbs touching that, being in the same boat, they allowed themselves to give nods of approval, seemingly expressing, "You scratch my back, I'll scratch yours. Two heads are better than one. We're in this through thick and thin to go the whole nine yards."

   So despite it all, the piners did witness more than one example where some trees demonstrated hospitality, offering shelter to the birds of the air and the little beasts of the park, and, bending over backwards, recognized that one good deed deserves another, including tolerating little human creatures crawling all over them.

   As gracious hosts to those who walked the paths among them, they seemed to be willing to even generously give an arm and a leg, a branch and a limb to take a back seat to humans, especially the ones that see the trees inhabiting the park as a close family, where even acorns don't fall far from the tree.

   The three piners, having been in on all that had gone on in the park community, left for the local coffee shop. There they discussed what they had discovered about trees and how they, too, resembled people, in all their array of characteristics. There, over coffee, they debated the merits of their distinct political stances, and how each would be relevant and help the residents of the park in a place which, though ridiculous in many ways, represents the planet, and all that is in it, and of which, they, too, are an integral part.

7

The Lake

The lake, like glass, often reflects the fashion statements of the trees that change their wardrobe to suit the seasons. Their beauty, no longer in colour, still shows as silhouettes against the full moon that, in glide path, sweeps its cool light across the drowsy lake.

Around the rocky shore line waves slap the rocks aggravated by the changing winds. Deep sighs or loud roars blast forth, then often the wind changes to heavy breathing, and finally sinks into a deep sleep interrupted only by a little smack or whistle. The wind never seems to suffer from insomnia, though, for somewhere around that lake it will violently stir the air, while at another place, where nature stretches its arms, the water will be calm. When nature does come awake after a midday nap and breathes heavy, its breath, smelling of juniper, and pine exudes a "muscular energy in sunlight corresponding to the spiritual energy of wind." [15]

That exhaling rush of wind often blew across the water where fountains, and in and outflows freshened the waters. Still the weeds grew, died, and rotted, making a mucky mess, the likes of which one park walker remembers, as a kid with his friends, dancing about covered from head to foot with mud and weeds.

A naive child might see muck as fun, but not so those who tried to head off the danger of the lake becoming a swamp or bog. Oh, so many tried! First, it was carp. Then with failure, a joking suggestion was made " to put a moose in there to gorge on the weeds." Then came the ultimate solution, dredge the damn lake, and be done with it - more depth, fewer weeds, no swamp, no bog.

Many interested souls, including college students, stretched their concern about the longevity of the lake to query what's under the lake. And what will their water testing results be?

Their bringing forth, dipping, peering, shaking, and staring at their precious jar-filled findings, was in one instance, supplied by a willing wader who brushed aside strangling weed to ensure group success. What would be the motive of someone willing to risk bleeding feet from broken glass, and sprained ankles from loss of balance on boulders lining the lake?

Those boulders and rocks, lining the lake like people, were different sizes, shapes, and colours. Had they not been so formidably heavy, they might have been carted away to cars and trucks that had patiently been waiting for their masters return. Had they not been so much in public view, and, if a mite smaller, collectors no doubt would have considered pocketing them, reveling in their beauty.

Leaning over the rails of one of the park's bridges, stretching and looking down past glossy trees and bulrushes, one could see more rocks, caged in wire mesh under the bridge, creating a barrier to water craft whose paddlers or rowers wished to augment the golf course small lagoon's furnishings with their intruding presence.

There were though, some examples of human behaviour

that just couldn't be controlled. There, an understanding of human curiosity and ingenuity caused park caretakers to show remarkable patience with those who, in winter, practiced their weight- lifting and curling skills by hurling stones out onto the ice where in the spring they sank out of place, leaving their former neighbour rocks to fend for themselves along the shore.

One regular in the park recalled the day when he found one particular and peculiar boulder that was left to fend for itself.

He was surprised one day as he was riding to a friend's on an old rail bed. The tracks had been torn up long before. He noticed a giant hamburger-shaped rock that, if he spread his arms out wide, they would barely touch its sides. Curious, he had a good look at it. Wonder of wonders! It looked just like a hamburger bun all right, ready to open up to put the mustard and ketchup in. Only it was grey. He borrowed his dad's crow bar and pried it open. It was incredible. The inside shone with shell-like rainbow colors. It was like a clam, only huge! His friend said he'd talk to the museum about it. He knew someone there. He thought they'd found an amazing thing, only to hear, " So what's new." A little later, as he gazed at that giant petrified mollusk, the rainbow shell colours, exposed to the air and light, faded to become dull and chalky. Another of life's disappointments!

With all those, must be a thousand rocks and boulders along the lake's shore of the park, there should be a few that hold surprises or secrets. Yet, as with people, it's not good to pry, especially in a park where so many who walk the paths, care for this place, seeing it as a real treasure, and so remain vigilant.

From the paths, across the grass, walking along side the boulders, one comes to a set of steps that surprisingly lead into more boulders. Once far in the past, they must have had a clear opening to the water before them. Now, like those whose decrepit limbs forgot their once usefulness, those steps remain as a reminder of some past time.

Further along one comes across a useful sloping concrete passage to shallow open water The sign nearby says, "Boat Ramp." Though it has the freedom to facilitate boat and canoe launching, very few use it. Had the lake been open to power boats, perhaps that would be a different story. One writer musing on modern preferences said:

"It's hard for the modern generation to understand Thoreau, who lived beside a pond but didn't own water skis or a snorkel." 16

It's also hard to imagine a lake that can't be jumped in for a swim. No high rocks to dive off into shallow water and become a paraplegic, no swimming out to a raft to sit beside a girl, and let fish nibble at your toes, but that's the way it is, But that's almost okay, because you can join the others' seal-like slippery bodies jumping into the park's swimming pool close by.

"Besides, you don't have to pay attention to the park's 'No Swimming' signs when the ice freezes over near the park's Goose Island, and a city worker's front-end loader shoves the snow aside like the parting of the Red sea for a skating rink." So said one regular park visitor. He risked most winters by edging up to the poles marking where you shouldn't go any further, "cause the ice isn't safe beyond that."

Though, throughout the winter, fliers , no doubt, could see from the air, footprints and ski tracks. But those soon faded as warm weather softened the ice, and as one said, "Spring's the time you have to be careful where you ice walk."

One older fellow, clucking under his breath, stopped, stared, and felt very uneasy watching a teenage girl feigning courage, step further out onto rubber-like ice sloshing with water, while two teen boys urged her on, their bravado seeping nervousness.

They had thrown her toque out onto the ice and then dared her to retrieve it. Tension grew. The boys began looking very uneasy. With strained expressions, they peered behind them, and from side to side, "sweating blood." their voices growing louder. What to do? The girl laughed, and scurried to the shore waving her wet hat in their faces. The old spectator, just shook his head, wiped his spectacles on his sleeve, and saw the three playfully kick and punch as they headed back to school.

When spring coaxed the candled ice to shatter sounding like crushing ice for a cool drink, many packed up their ice fishing gear, and dug out their casting rods and lures. The harsh winter fishing was replaced with the more sedate version of the sport much applauded. One enthusiast even said:

"God never did make a more calm, quiet, innocent recreation than angling. " [17]

Among many who watched fathers and sons, mothers, and daughters, and others, casting their lures from the shore, hoping for a jack fish, yellow perch, or even sucker, was a fellow fascinated with the whole business, especially when some cast into the wind, reeled in weeds, or tried to yank their lines, taut as a guitar string, free before they broke.

The fellow, a grandfather, missed his distant grandchildren whom he had hoped to talk about how he'd made his own fishing lures, netted minnows, helped his dad bury dead suckers(carp) in the garden for fertilizer, fillet the good fish and fry them over a camp fire.

His thought-bubble burst. He coaxed his stiff joints to stand, stepped over to one of the park's floating docks, reached down with his cane and poked at a bloated fish floating belly up, its orange fins waving at him. "They say, the ice conditions were such that many fish perished from oxygen starvation. Maybe that was so."

Out on the water beyond the dock, on good days, and even when the winds stirred the water into a frenzy, shouts, and laughter, and a drum beat could often be heard from dragon boats heading for or around red buoys. Those big balls bobbing about, were much different from the rubber-tired, hip-wadered fishermen, who didn't seem to mind curious stares from shore.

Canoers hardly got a second glance. The once-in -awhile park worker's boat, outboard engine driven, ruffled a few feathers of the "obey the rule folk." But other than that, the water was reserved mostly for a few fish, water fowl, a muskrat or two, and their natural predators.

Oh, there was the floating water debris that sometimes looked like a body, but it was later found to be a garbage bag.

8

The Foreboding Visitor

The lamp light shone onto the side of the rough-barked aging tree. Beyond, down the path, narrowed by the golf course and Japanese garden chain link fences, walked a lone figure. A sudden flapping noise above his head, somewhere in the twisted branches of a tree, stopped him cold. He listened and looked. Then hearing only the spewing of water into the frigid air above the golf course pond, he shrugged and began again his shuffle toward the opening onto the parking lot, bordered by a busy road.

The next day the walker passed a couple coming up on the mouth of the path. It was six a.m. The breeze rippled the water. Ducks, that bobbed about the day before, hid in the shadowed scum near the rocks. The couple paused and pointed. At what? The walker looked, " What was that on the tree top?"

"Too big for a flicker or crow, and it isn't an owl."
 "No, it couldn't be!"
"Yes, it's an eagle. That's strange. Must have lost its way."
"No, I heard some are over at the other park's lake

that's nowhere near as big as this one. The city is having some eagle visitors."

A week's worth of sun rising and setting saw the walker frequently stopping and asking couples if they'd seen the eagle in flight. For that yellow billed, frowning tufted head dignified its body, balanced motionlessly high above the walker's head. Did anyone photograph that intruder in the act of swooping off with a gosling in its cruel talons? The walker hadn't heard. All he knew was that one day when he stopped by the tree - the eagle's perch, the bird was gone. He thought back into his childhood, remembering walking a wider path, a road, and seeing the Case company tractor globe symbol topped off with an eagle whose wings also remain unspread. As an imaginative child he had hoped that it, too, would spread its mighty wings and take flight. It never happened. The disappointments of life accumulated in his memory clusters, to await the coming of an eagle or nature's other surprises. Thus, the present never escapes the past.

9

Chosen Goslings

The water splashers, and the winged air movers, that includes geese, assert their place in nature's scheme of things, and so it holds true that,
"When one tugs at a single thing in nature, he finds it attached to the rest of the world." [18]

Those attached in the park, the water birds, like geese, ducks and gulls, are busy all through the day, unlike soaring hawks and eagles which rarely spread their wings early in the morning. They usually wait until the sun warms the air enough to catch the rising air currents [19]

What a picture! Staring up into the sky, one can marvel at the gliding grace and nodding necks of the predators whose natural mission to kill can be overlooked when mesmerized by their aerial displays. Oh, if only their prey could demonstrate such finesse. But, whether we like it or not,
"In nature, the emphasis is in what is rather than what

ought to be." [20]

That's so true. For park visitors need resign themselves to the raucous squawking on Goose Island , the ridiculous peeping from adolescent geese who should by now offer decent honks, and the goose droppings. They also must share space with sociable geese lounging on the golf course, and the intimidating hesitation of geese arrogantly strutting about on the paths.

With such blatant behaviour, it seems not out of order to share the remark of one passing by a small flock, some clambering over the rocks onto the path. She turned to her companion, saying,
"My, they're tempting. They should be on the dinner table instead of flaunting their attributes."

Geese wearing their down-filled vests do make their presence known with their nasal voices, V-ing to or hustling back after scrounging farmers' grain.

The kerrfuffle of their noisy efforts intensifies when grey, heavy skies, ice-crystaled air, and open frigid water succumbs to glassy ice crusts. Then anxious geese raise their bellies, slap the water to keep it open while honking complaints. So it is, when the lake gets congested with geese, and there doesn't seem as if any room is left on the water for others, circling, trying to land - the noises of the those who already laid claim to their water rights is deafening. One person taking in the drama, asked another, "What's going on?" The other, " Those on the water are telling the ones in the air to SCRAM!"

Sadness about seeing the necessity of this annual repeat performance just doesn't enter the minds of most park visitors, for no doubt they agree with one who said,

"To be interested in the changing seasons is a happier state of mind than to be hopelessly in love with spring." 21

For when nature packs away one suit of colourful clothing, and brings out another - repeating it four times in its park living room, it makes, not only a fashion statement, but it shouts down the hall papered in calendar months, "Get with it, change is good. "

So the geese, along with other migrating birds, sometimes grounded by low ceilings, other times free to fly high through open skies, yearly remind us of our need to adjust to changing conditions. That's life.

But, sometimes these athletic, gung-ho geese take the easy way out, and succumb to becoming feathered couch potatoes. If truth be told they no longer park in long lines like beads on water in a migration mood, but rather, throw their lot in with other pesky birds. You see,

" Sometimes birds learn to exploit modern ecological alternatives - gulls thrive at garbage dumps and migrant shore birds are found at sewage beds." 22

Now how can that come about, when it comes to those "V" formation flyers?

The park sign "PLEASE DON'T FEED THE GEESE" leads to the answer.

Migrant birds, like geese can become dependant on handouts from people, and so stop foraging, "waiting for food to come to them," leaving them too weak to migrate even if they wanted too. Moldy bread, fruit, instead of their natural foods, left overs from "feed the geese sessions to help and amuse both geese and people" is bad news for geese. It causes them to be, "Hanging around instead of migrating as they're supposed to do." 23

It seems that these water fowl do know they are safe from hunters when plunked down on the park's lake. But, move on they must.
That primeval instinctive behaviour in dramatic form, not only is something to behold, even though it's a predictable annual event, but it leaves human spectators with the unfinished business of trying to answer some ragged around the edges questions posed by children less familiar with the performance.

When the birds on the water are in a restless mood, and it looks like they're ready to head south, how do they know when that moment has come? Who decides? One leader, or more than one?

Why the "V"? Why don't they just take off, and each do its own thing?

Some adult spouted out a college Sociology 101 course answer,
" Watching geese in formation, and the birds taking turns in the lead position is an example of what should happen in groups. There is a need to spell off leaders, giving them a break by taking a backseat position, at least for a while."
Others, having done some reading in ornithology answered in another way,

"A few large birds like geese...and pelicans are frequently seen flying in "V " formations or in straight lines. The advantage of flying this way is still being argued, but each bird behind the leader may get a little bit of lift from the flap of the bird in front of it, or the flap of the bird in front may create a vacuum making the upstroke easier for the next bird." 24

All the academic mental gymnastics still leaves most who frequent the park with a haunting feeling that there is more that touches them at a deeper level when in company with nature's flying miracles.

"The natural creature has only two primal passions, to get and beget." [25]

Two geese, unlike the others in the flock who preened and proudly displayed their "recently- hatched," bobbed about looking confused. In the following weeks more and more ganders left their female partners to look after their broods. Some mothers just couldn't cope with big families. Some young ones, smaller and weaker than most, just couldn't figure out how to feed and stay out of trouble. It looked like, sooner or later, they would be snatched up by the grasping claws of diving owls or eagles, or yanked under by sharp toothed fish. Even if, with rapid growth in days ahead, their frantic flapping and splayed, webbed feet could break free to join stretch-necked honking conversationalists, who plow-shared their way through sleet and fog, could they keep up, having had a poor start in life? Even if that happened, would they, ill prepared, survive hunters' blue steel blasts to circle and glide to a peaceful end?

Those questions mingled with the moist mist of dawn as the gosling-less couple cautiously dared to shorten the honking distance between them and mothers frantically trying to corral their overpopulated gaggle of curious peepers.

The couple's deep voicings, and gently swaying necks with hesitating feathering seemed to reassure the moms that no harm would come to them or their brood. The couples' signals only begged the moms to let them, as gosling-less, have two or three of their goslings to raise. Even the smaller, weaker would be fine. For their own hatching never happened, and they longed to see little peeping balls of feathers grow into splashing awkward, voice-changing adolescents, and finally into strong, mean-business hissing and honking adult Canadian geese.

The goslings had needs. What was best for them, and also for the new adoptive mother and proud gander? So much had happened. The gander had run a flight school for beginners who hadn't yet earned their wings and had no idea how to fly in "v" formation. It was that year his life-long partner hatched no eggs. Having no hope of another hatching that year or ever, the couple decided to try to adopt the three goslings.

A question asked by an onlooker, as the would- be parents swam in among the big bunch of newly hatched was, "Would the couple show that they had preferences? Or would they just pick out the first three they swam close to? " It looked like it didn't matter what the size, colour, or amount of feathers the goslings showed as they bobbed about. Any three would receive their love and attention.

There was yet one thing left to do though. The adopting couple had to pass some tests to prove they were worthy to bring the adopted up to flying speed to clear the water with the flock and eventually head south. Feeding was important. Could they get the attention of the goslings they had in mind to adopt, to learn how to find just the right weedy spots to dip their bills down in the water to feed? Would the gander stay around to help the mother with goslings, or would he toot off with the boys, leaving the goose to raise their newly adopted? Did the new soon-to- be parents have a call that their goslings would pay attention to, even when the little rascals were too busy doing their own things away from mom and dad? Would the parents demonstrate honks and other mom and dad sounds that could be sorted out as different from the rest of the flock? All these questions and more had to be answered before the adopting parents could take charge of their new brood.

So, before the couple could swim away with their three goslings, the mothers in charge of their day care had to still wave their beaks in approval. In the meantime, the parents to be, had permission to swim about nearby. Weeks passed. But then the day care "in charge" mom's neck swayed an invitation for the couple to swim close, to goose talk.

It appeared that the day care bosses had three other goslings in mind than the three the couple had preened with their bills as the ones they wanted. The couple were led over to three others. The day care bosses waved their necks, splashed the water with their wings, circled about in the water, all to entice the couple to take the three they had counted on the couple considering.

It appeared that the couple had passed the tests to be parent geese. But the three the day care bosses had chosen for them, why, they were bigger, and older, and out of hand behaviour-wise. The on looker to this drama wondered whether the new parents were viewed as too old in the coal black eyes of the day care bosses, and maybe it was thought they'd not be able to survive the hunters' gun blasts to last through the years it would take for the first- choice three to become able to fly and fend for themselves. No, it was not that. For the flock would somehow care for the little ones left orphaned if the worst came to worst. Besides, the time to fly south and leave the park haven was months away.

The couple, not wanting to give the impression that they were too old to care for little ones, put their heart in soul in demonstrating their swimming, flying, feeding, and fending off intruder skills. They swooped, dipped, dived, performed extraordinary arial acrobatic skills, and hissed, and made darn-right nuisances of themselves, pecking and poking their neighbours. They did, indeed, look sincere in their intentions. Finally, those making the big decision threw up their wings in surrender, stopped dragging their web feet through the water, and nodded with their bills to where the couple were to pick up their three babies.

The couple wagged their tails, waved their long necks, touched their blue bills, chattered, gave a polite, sedate honk or two and running across the water gracefully lifted off. The morning sun shone on their white jaw patches, the tips of their broad fanned black and grey wings effortlessly flapped, signalled satisfaction and sheer pleasure.

Soon the two hovered over the mud banked creek, its murky water, like glass, mirroring a dark reflection of the two dropping to meet the glassy surface. Three little fuzz balls paddled under the bridge gently herded by a matronly goose. At last the moment arrived, the couple would be united with their three adopted.

The onlooker thought well, that's it. They shall live happy ever after. But then, the matronly escort had the last word before disappearing under the bridge and out of sight. One of the babies looked a little sickly. The onlooker imagined, in watching the escort gaggling away accompanied by splashing and wing gestures, that the escort could be warning them that the little one suffered from some chronic bird chest condition. They, as goose parents, would have their hands full trying to keep that sickly one alive. One could hear a little dry cough, and see the little fellow labouring to catch his breath. But, despite the warnings the couple without question wanted the little gosling. He had a sad look. The gosling got its little beak pointed in the right direction, aimed right for the couple. Its tiny web feet paddled frantically while it leaned to reach the circle of safety around the couple. The other two goslings had already nestled in close to their new mom and dad. The "sickly" gosling perked up as the two grown-ups embraced him, but when they turned their attention to feeding and began to join the flock in the big water under the bridge, the little urchin began peeping in the most pathetic way, leaving his new parents to return and once again embrace him reassuringly.

The couple with their three goslings set out to join up with their own flock far down the lake. It wasn't an easy journey. The three little ones webbed feet sometimes got tangled up in weeds as they hugged the shoreline ready at any time to huddle in the shadows of the rocks lining the lake. Where the parent geese could break the surface of the water at a running pre flight gate, their little charges had to struggle along looking very vulnerable. Through sunrise and sunset and into the cool darkness of night the family warily made its way. When the sun lifted its head out of the grey morning haze to cast a warm glow on the birds backs, they arrived to be greeted by warming sun. The mom and dad, so elated at having got their brood safely home, lifted their bodies into the air. Soaring, dipping their wings, circling, they honked a delightful duet. Then, having roused the drowsy and sleeping heads from under wings, they swooped down and landed, coasting up to their goslings, just like a float plane taxies up to waiting ones.

Where humans would wave and cast gesturing reflections on glassy surfaces surrounding docks, the tired little goslings and their parents were greeted by nose blowing noises of a splashing, tail wiggling gaggle of geese so bent on well wishing that they almost lost their graceful water-sifting dignity, leaving them appearing embarrassed.

Four of the five family members found feather touching, diplomatic honks, peeps, and ripple web foot wiggling worked well in gaining acceptance by the flock. But one energetic gosling, the older of the three, just couldn't put his best web foot forward. He pleasantly surprised his mom and dad geese by trying to fly with few-feathered, baby wing stumps. The youngster, when not stirring up the waters to imitate his adopted parents, was stirring things up by pestering the patient ganders, who now and then would hiss and peck at him, out-doing anything he did to ruffle their feathers. He, eventually, not getting anywhere with the grown-ups, spun his fluffy body about, twisting and turning and elbowing his sister and brother as he peeped and pestered, pestered and peeped, getting them to scurry over to their mother.

The honking orchestra, familiar to human bystanders, would settle in to give renditions of its usual domestic bliss. Then feathers would fly. Why? Because the little guy, who, having swum around with wing limbs tucked under his feathers, looking lonely and bored, nudged his way into the crowd, and when given a gentle push or two, lost his temper, hissed, and attacked the biggest gander who had his back turned. It seemed the little gosling just couldn't let things be. He appeared to have to keep pushing to see how far he could go, to see what would happen if he disturbed the way things were in the flock. He even nipped the tail feathers on a mighty big guard gander, one which usually stood guard when most were head down nibbling on grass, sleeping, or gossiping. His mother would often swim over to him, let him snuggle up, then he'd push at her and paddle away, distancing himself from her show of affection.

It wasn't long before the gosling's mother and dad began fussing about, honking, chasing and herding back their restless one while trying to soothe the ruffled feathers of those troubled by their little one. He was a cute little thing, and the onlooker saw some female aunty-like birds fuss over him. But though the water was brown and tepid, things were heating up in the usually sociable flock, with the trouble generated by the new family's still unhappy gosling. It looked like things just wouldn't work out where they were. Then the onlooker, concerned for the newly formed family, was relieved. He saw a big gander lead the family away from the flock now almost in turmoil. The family of five followed in his wake, down the lake to where another flock noisily neighboured together.

By then, the family looked very weary. The onlooker imaged the family members might feel more comfortable with the new flock. It looked like a real mix of birds of all shapes, sizes and shades of grey mixed with white. There were a number of ducks, they too a real mix, swimming among the geese. The newly adopting parents were of one breed of geese, their adopted gosling, of another. So, perhaps in the new flock, things would work out better. Maybe. Though it looked like the troubled little gosling suddenly realized that the other two, his new sister and brother, weren't going anywhere. Despite his peeping, hissing, and other throaty sounds, that together sounded like "Goslings go home now," his slow head down, sorrowful swimming about gave the onlooker the idea that that little creature realized he'd have to share or compete with his new brother and sister for the attention of his parents.

That first night among the second flock, all but one of the family of five melded themselves into sleeping shapes looking like pebbles or rocks. Throughout the night and well into the early morning hours, the troubled one's brother began sleeping almost under the wings of his mother. But that didn't last long. Soon he feather-puffed his way onto the slimy weeded space between some shore rocks. His mother retrieved him, bill nudging him back to the safety of the flock. This drifting away and escorting back went on for hours, despite his mother's efforts to limit his restless movements to the circle of safety.

The little urchin of a gosling, unlike his older brother and younger sister goslings, looked bedraggled. His feather coat looked mottled. His little head looked flea-bitten, and his gangly legs and web feet toed inward, a sight for sore eyes. Veteran ganders of many flights through shot-gun pellet sprayed corridors and hail thrashings, couldn't look worse than the newly adopted middle-child gander. Still the onlooker said to himself, "What a beautiful gosling!"

The ragged little gosling continued his restless sleeping habits in his new home. Many suns rose and set, and in time he began hoisting himself on water- lapped slippery rocks along the shore. He and his brother used nature's playground equipment, rocks and reeds, weeds and the odd floating log to test their strength. The older, though a bit smaller, used his speed and cunning to play. In the eyes of the bystander, he didn't play fair. Maybe by Goose rules that was okay. But the younger, whose voice was changing from a meek peep, to a raspy broken honk, let it be known, having got most of the cuffs and bumps, that he was frustrated.

Yet the two did show they had mutual interests. They seemed to enjoyed the interesting mix of noise bill vibrations that ricocheted off the rocks, trees, and which they tried to imitate. Through tail wagging, stirring up the water they expressed great delight in making a contribution to noisy nose sounds punctuated by geese feeding and burping honks.

The other adolescent geese including some mallard ducks often came and played with the three who appeared different even from them.

The onlooker thought the visitor to the adopted parents' patch of water seemed surprised, as did their grown-up escort when the older of the three did something unusual for a goose. Seeing a dog on the path by the waters edge, instead of saying "Woof, woof." which would in itself be unusual for a goose to honk, he stretched open his beak, and out came what sounded like "Kingmiuk." The surprised onlooker remembered that word was an approximation of the Inuit word for dog. He thought, well, that little creature is honking in Canadian, as the name of his specie indicates. Though perhaps that word would be more appropriate coming out of the throat of a snow goose, rather than a Canadian goose.

Suppose the little creature had been adopted by a snow goose passing through. Would he have spent more time in the Arctic, assimilated into the local snow goose culture? Maybe he'd intermarry and raise Canadian Snow Geese. That wouldn't be too far fetched. But then, would he be accepted by his adopted parents geese family? One wonders.

The onlooker could see that the mother of the adopted three, was particularly showing concern and fear for the safety of her brood; especially one dark moonless night. When the stillness was broken by the sound of powerful predators' wings above the water, the mother began frantically swimming and honking about, searching for her three. Her two teenage males had been wandering off on their own more frequently, foraging further away each day. Now, though, wasn't the time to assert their independence. They no doubt might have gone to their death under the claws of night prowlers overhead, as many had before, had it not been for their mother who spotted one, and then the other two, and nudged them back into the shelter of the rocks.

The goose looked agitated not only when conscious of dangers without, but also those within her three goslings. The motley, bedraggled little one, though gangling and rugged, was falling behind on their family outings in search of food among the weeds and other water plants. The young gosling often would shake his head as if to rid himself of something that didn't belong within him. He'd repeatedly give a half-hearted honk, but it was as if he didn't give a hoot. His heart just wasn't with it. He was obviously ill, and becoming weaker. Others with the same symptoms often died, their putrefying bodies floating about like dead fish bellied up in the froth along the lake shore.

The goose, somehow seemed to know that she couldn't cure her sick one. Leading her three along the shore, stopping often to let her sick one catch up, she finally swam into the shallows with her brood. Humans passing by along the water edge path may have noticed the mother with two healthy goslings, and a sickly one nudged by its mother up onto the lake's boat ramp where it layed sprawling. The mother didn't look surprised or concerned when a passing human on the path gently picked it up, cradled it in her hands, warmed it up inside her jacket and headed for her car. The mother goose did not look surprised either, when weeks later, the same human returned and gently set her absentee gosling back in the water where she and her other two goslings were feeding. Nor was the mother surprised when her gosling wagged its tail feathers, flapped its wings, twisted its neck and head in swaying motions, and rushed over to give his siblings an affectionate peck or two each.

The onlooker though, "Well, I'll be darned. Had other feathered friends connected in similar, profound mysterious ways with humans?"

The raw instinct to survive played out every moment on the lake and by the shore. Dogs took humans for walks along the path bordering the shore. Geese and ducks loitered and casually pecked and dipped under for morsels of bugs, and choice bits of weed. Some geese flew, or scrambled and hopped over the rocks to strut about, arching their long necks down to stretch and nibble at the grass under the watchful eye of a towering-necked gander.

A dog dancing merrily down the path, might come to a lurching halt, lean forward, sometimes bark, sniff the air and twang its leash to get at the geese. Then geese, not wanting to appear undignified, with heads up, would slowly land-paddled toward the water, seemingly refusing to lose their graceful composure. Where dogs often acted uncouth, the geese portrayed a royal presence till they hit the water, and with a frenzy flurry of flapping wings distanced themselves from dogs and their human companions.

While the open water gave the gun-shy geese an opportunity to feel safe - the boulders lining the lake, gave dogs and humans the chance to play the game of hop, and slip, lose balance, and even sprain or break an ankle or a leg. Attentive to keeping their footing they often lost all interest in departing ducks and geese.

Dogs could be a blessing or a curse, the onlooker thought. He remembered being up north where dogs sometimes ran wild, Then, they were some sources of danger for children. Many local dogs often ran loose in packs, and when the winds blew strongly, they seemed to become more vicious. Stories were told of packs of dogs killing children, or maiming them for life.

Dogs frequenting the park were usually well controlled, less a danger to people than to geese. Once, before the father gander went off with the other ganders, leaving the mother and goslings to fend for themselves, a huge long-haired husky sniffed around the water's edge. Though it did not venture onto the boulders , it did do what huskies do. It howled and howled. That got attention of the gander who hadn't heard that sound up close before. His only acquaintance was with hunting dogs, especially retrievers, some who couldn't tell the difference between a dead or alive duck. The gander eventually lost interest in the big dog, and the dog lost interest in the gander and his family. But it didn't lose interest in doing what sled dogs do. It yanked and pulled on its leash, no doubt imagining that it was pulling a sled. Its petite female owner all but flew through the air, as he took her for a run down the path.

After the gander left, the goose found a safe secluded spot in the pool fed by water running under the path. There, like any housebound mom, with dad away, she kept her three close by, watching their play often end up in feathers flying, and the murky water muddying up their feathered coats.

The onlooker thought about parents where one was often away, like the gander who left the goose to care for the goslings. He imagined that if geese could think like human creatures they might have recalled, as he did, much that was told of what happened when one parent was away from family.

He thought back to one family that he knew about. The geese, the park, and the lake reminded him of them and what they had faced. The park and its inhabitants continued to evoke other thoughts of other times, and other places.

10

Lone Wild Goose

A lone wild goose seemed frozen in nature's photo frame. Water lapped at its tuxedo dressed chest. But rather than a debonair, proud, in command presence, its plaintive, pathetic bill vibrations moved through the still air, reaching across the water to Goose Island and throngs of gossiping noisy couples.

Gander or goose, no matter, the walker paused in his steps down the path, stared at the lonely bird, and felt pity, thinking how that creature had lost its mate, and how its loss affected its place in the flock that appeared indifferent to its mournful cry of despair.

A walker thought of how that lone bird's predicament could be compared to that of a person who, having lost his or her spouse through death, no longer enjoyed the company of friends who knew them as a couple. Now it was different. In the company of couples, the goose was the odd one out. The friends didn't quite know what to do with the survivor, and that bereaved one's new awkwardness showed.

A disturbance above the walker's head rescued him from such morbid thought. He searched the heavy blanket of clouds. A low flying flock broke through into sight, descended and landed across the lake among the gossiping flock.

The walker looked beyond the lonely bird towards that mobile community of geese, and formed a picture in his mind of the tragic event when the lone goose lost its mate.

A thirteen year old opened the four by four's passenger door, sat. Silence, then a pout changed to a wide grin, then a, "Whoopee! I got it. Look dad, I passed the test. I can now shoot that 12 gauge."
"When are ya going to go after them."
"Tomorrow, Saturday."
"Great!"

No alarm clock was needed. The boy was up. He groped through the dark room toward the open window. The cold tingled. Beyond the bare, tortured looking trees, just above the silhouetted house tops, a blood red ribbon of light slowly took on width and warm colours blending in with the still gun steel grey of sky.

Down the stairs, into the kitchen, into the fridge reaching for milk, his eagerness abruptly ended. when he was surprised by a voice.
"Bacon and eggs, toast, the works; it's on the table, sit down son." Today, he was to be initiated as a man. Man's breakfast, man's hunt and shoot together. Before it was man, boy; boy tagging along, to fetch and carry. Soon he'd smite the dawn air with lead pellets tearing into warm flesh to bloody the ground, or be washed away among reeds in murky stagnant water. Soon, maybe, he'd wade among living and dead water growth to seek out a broken winged creature sqeezing its body into the murky mess to die.

In they flew, in formation, circling. The rush of air and wide flapping wings broke the silence. Two crouched waiting, gun barrels sticking upward. The boy tensed up, His dad, grasping the denim of his shoulder whispered, "Wait. Not yet; Now!" The boy sprang upward. He barely heard, " Pick one, give it some lead, swing, SHOOT!" felt the 12 gauge recoil kick.

"Dad, dad, I got it. It's falling. It's there. Look over there. Still flapping, splashing. Shoot it again?"

"No, go get it, by the neck."

He waded out, stared down at the contorted bone, blood, and twisted-winged creature of the air, now a helpless mess. Reaching down to grab it. he pulled his hands away; He stared at the hissing snapping bill, then lurching, grabbed its neck, and staggered towards his dad, the heavy body swinging and slapping hard against his tired legs. Strong hands took the once beautiful bird, grasped its neck, swung it around, and dropped the dead thing to the ground.

The boy looked up at his dad's grin and dutifully matched it with a faint smile. Now, he was a man. He wasn't sure. He felt a little queasy, faint, his appetite to eat game gone, given over to a question, killing, or hunting?

Above the heads of the man and his young companion, the flock, one short, flew on honking to each other to keep in touch. One craned its neck, searching around in the V for its life long partner, its changing intonations getting no familiar returning sounds. The grey dawn gave way to warming sun. By mid-day the flock approached the lake, honked in chorus, giving notice to the others beaded out on the water, calling out, "Make room." As the birds circled, the lone goose broke from the noisy lot and dropped down on the other side of the lake to swim alone, giving out unending pleading calls for its mate, puzzled and in despair at its partner's disappearance.

The persistent honking broke into the walker's daydream, leaving him with a haunting question.

"Could the boy hunter know or even understand in his

bonding with his dad, how he had severed the bond between two others of nature's creatures?"

11

Ducks and Others

"Nature is an endless combination and repetition of a very few laws. She hums the old well known air through innumerable variations." [26]

"Mallards and coots don't winter where they breed. In spring they usually return to where they were born, or to where they were before heading south. Males usually arrive first, and begin rehearsing their singing and showmanship that will improve their chances of getting a mate when the females arrive. With some early arrivals, like Red- winged Blackbirds, many weeks may pass before the females show up. Males arriving first are ones that defend their territory where mating and nesting take place. The females may not arrive until there is enough food around for them to form eggs. By then the males have already set up their territories and can get on with the business of courting and wooing." [27]

Sounds familiar, as when a spouse gets transferred to another city, and goes first to get things set up before the partner arrives with the children. That also seemed to occur when, in the settling of Canada, male emigrants arrived first.

"When it came to the Arctic, and ducks breeding, things were different. Both males and females arrived together from the south since the breeding season is very short. There isn't much time for preliminaries like courtship. Ducks wintered down south together, but pairs always returned to the female's place of birth. That made sense since females would then be familiar with the areas where they would nest and singlehandedly raise the young." [28]

That's not too uncommon today with humans, and a bit like it was in biblical times where the husband settled in with the wife's family for awhile after they married. Then, again, there's also the male thing where, like geese , many dads go off to be with the boys, leaving the moms to care for the kids.

Demonstrations of duck moms conscientiously caring for their broods, in one instance surfaced in a most remarkable scene. Picture this, it actually happened. On the park boat ramp near the shallow water a mother duck bobbed about in front of her ducklings. That in itself isn't unusual. What is, though, is that the ducklings, standing on the edge of the boat ramp, side by side in a perfect line, looked very attentively at their mother. It was as if she were a school teacher, instructing her class on the finer points of being a duck.

Uncommon occurrences among ducks were very rare. Usually, there they were, either mingling in with the geese on the water, standing asleep on rocks, mucking in the weeds, or diving, often with their rumps up, mooning the public. A few couples, even the odd Mallard pair, perhaps fascinated with golf, chose small ponds on the golf course in which to mate and mingle, but most looked more comfortable on the lake where the geese chose to swim.

There may have been a good reason for that. "Many

water birds, both soarers and flappers depend on the wind to become airborne, and often have difficulty taking off from the ground when they cannot drop off a high perch. Ducks and coots, must run on the water into the wind, flapping their wings, to take to the air. Other ducks, such as Mallards, that live in marshes or small ponds where they can be surprised suddenly without room for a running takeoff, have evolved the ability to jump right into the air." 29

    Park ducks, less jumpy than those who chose the wild, not intimidated by human presence when interrupted on shore or near it, merely, like the geese, snubbed the onlookers coming too close, turned their backs, and slowly swam away.

    It's a different kettle of fish when it comes to noisy terns. There's no nonchalant, casual feeding approach here. Terns do arial surveys seeking their dinners. That may even explain why for the most part they dress in white dinner jackets.

"…many seabirds are partly or almost entirely white, the colour visible at greatest distance in all light conditions…by being white, a feeding gull can be seen by other gulls far away. They can stop searching and join the one who has found food enough for many." 30

    Terns' invasion of the park picnic places is like that of a bunch of excited teenagers descending upon a fast food outlet. There do not seem to be too many sedate slow flyers and hoppers among those terns that soar, dip, dive, and swoop down upon the park . Perhaps it's because they are for the most part tern teenagers, free of family responsibilities. The fact is that "terns don't nest until the third year after their birth." 31

    So they can afford to be playful, and even aggressive. It wasn't unusual to see a gang of short hopping terns even take on a persistent pesky black crow, forcing it to yield and give up its place at a picnic table.

The terns and crows table manners were a far cry from those other birds in Goose Island Park. Joining the neighbourhood regulars: the crows, terns, ducks, geese, coots, Northern Shovellers, Scaups, flickers that tapped on metal light posts, a pelican was a dignified visitor.

Every so often, without calling ahead, or getting an invitation it would make its appearance, sometimes with a female friend. Unlike mallards and geese that had only three toes joined with webbing, it had all four joined together with webbing. Usually it would gather on water with others of its kind to drive a school of fish into the shallows where they'd scoop them up.

The mystery of why this particular pelican and its mate would honour the park with its presence, unaccompanied by the rest of its community, went unsolved.

One person walking in the park, finding a dead bird on the path, and seeing that beautiful pelican drifting about on the lake, wondered whether other members of the pelican community were vulnerable or falling prey to the same stressors that confronted many other water fowl. He, no doubt, had heard it said that,

"Many people are directly concerned with the life histories of ducks, geese…and other game birds which must be known to assure that only a replaceable number are taken each year by hunters and that there are adequate refuges throughout the birds ranges. Food requirements, migration routes, tolerance of disturbance, nesting success, and other factors are all important in deciding when and where man can pursue these birds without damage to their populations." [32]

That in mind, he became sensitive to the fragility of life among his fellow creatures that included the birds of the air in the park and elsewhere.

12

The Bird At the Window

Winter had come to the prairies. The storm pelted the window with sleet and snow as the man settled before the crackling logs in his fireplace to read. Soon a thud, thud on his window pane brought him back to think of the night outside. A near frozen, panic-stricken bird darted desperately at his fire and crashed into the window, time and time again. The man opened the door to let the bird come into his warm home. But the wild thing could not understand and wouldn't fly in.

Leaving his warm farm house the man opened his shed door and lit a small heater in the shed, hoping to lure the bird into there. Still, it refused to come inside from the storm. He tried and tried, but it would not come in. Really frustrated, the man called out angrily,

"Oh, if only I could be a bird for one minute so that I could show you what I've been trying to tell you."

13

Best Friends, Kind Of

"Gentlemen of the Jury: The one, absolute, unselfish friend that man can have in this selfish world, the one that never deserts him, the one that never proves ungrateful or treacherous, is his dog. " [33]

Flying feathered creatures, unlike the dogs that took their masters for walks through the park most days, those birds just didn't quite have the same relationship and level of understanding as did these canine quadrupeds with their two-legged mammals friends. In fact, as one person wrote:

"The more one comes to know men, the more one comes to admire the dog." [34]

One can admire dogs for their patience with humans, and their sense of companionship. Often a passerby on the path would see a dog sitting beside its owner on a park bench, both looking out over the water. Sometimes one could even see a dog playing frisbee with its counterpart athlete, a human, one that discovered that dogs can not only be fun, but that they willingly accommodate other's needs.

An author, recognizing that one quality among many, wrote,

"The more I see the representatives of the people, the more I love my dogs." 35

Those who meet up with dogs and the friendly bodies at the other end of the leashes, learn that dogs serve many roles in human society. Dogs, besides being conversational pieces, God forbid, are like children who at times are vehicles for introducing people to each other. How often have conversations begun with, or among strangers, generated by a sincere interest in each others' dogs. Can't you just see it. Two strangers pass. Normally they might ignore each other. But each has a dog. So they stop, begin to compare notes about their pets while their dogs sit back, and, you'd swear, grin with satisfaction, having found a new friend or acquaintance for their human companion.

"No one appreciates the very special genius of your conversation as much as the dog does. Who loves me loves my dog." 36

Dogs also seem to have the magical ability to even warm up what would otherwise be a tense time among family members. One onlooker saw a bunch of family members charging down the path, obviously very upset with each other, and even with the world. If looks could kill, well...

Surprisingly, well, no, not really, a little later, following some distance behind, another family appeared. The children skipping along, parents smiling, arms around each others shoulders, stopping now and then to laugh at their little dog's shenanigans.

In the park, it was also made clear that dogs not only offer themselves as objects to laugh at, or to laugh with, but also offer themselves as creatures to help us laugh at ourselves. Never forgotten was the sight of a little dog being pulled in a wagon. "He's tired," said his smiling owner.

"The greatest pleasure of a dog is that you may make a fool of yourself with him and not only will he not scold you, but he will make a fool of himself too." 37

One person resting on a bench followed with his eyes a few persons and their dogs making the rounds of the park's lake. He remembered the dogs he had known.

Skippy was a black and white terrier that was "fixed." He got fatter and fatter, about a foot wide in the middle, and his legs seemed to grow shorter and shorter. Sometimes he even had to be pried out from behind the stove, his favorite sleeping spot. After he had done his business outside, he was helped up the stairs, and lifted into the house. It wasn't fun for him, nor for us. When he was younger and thinner the dad tried to give him away. He drove him way across the city, but Skippy somehow kept finding his way back, dodging traffic and mean kids all the way home. So he was kept.

The person on the park bench thought, I never had that yearning to come home when I left. I wasn't sure whether mom or dad really would have wanted me back. Yet I do remember my dad saying, when I left, that my room would always be there if I wanted it.

His thoughts drifted to Charlie. Old Charlie was another family dog, a pug. He replaced Rusty, a family dog who went senile. Poor Rusty snapped, bit, and often stared into space, standing rigidly on all four legs as if hypnotized. Charlie, on the other hand, was a real gentleman. He remembered vividly how he got Charlie. He had driven into a farm yard. Stepping out of the car, he heard a tea kettle whistling sound. Looking around, he finally saw the source. There lying snoring was what he first thought to be a teenage pot bellied pig. Yet when it opened its eyes, he could clearly see that it was a bulging eyed "Pug." The farmer working in the yard told him that was Charlie. He remembered saying to the farmer,

"Looks like a great pet."

The farmer asked, " Do you want umm?"

He was surprised and asked, "You're giving him away?" and the farmer said, "Sure, if you want umm, you can have umm. No use around here!"

Charlie joined the family, wagging his curly pig tail, snuffling and snorting. He would skitter about the house with his toe nails scratching away at the floor to get a good grip. So bashful, he would only drop his guard when us kids were at school. Then he'd nuzzle up a bit of fluff from the floor, and proudly prance about, balancing it on the ridge of his nose. Sadly Charlie died.

Unlike either of these dogs, two who appeared in the park had other ideas of what play was all about. The first was either marooned on the park's Goose Island, with strange ideas of what would benefit him. Or, tantalized by the geese fussing about on the Island he thought he'd swim over and enjoy a good dinner. How he got there was one thing, but, in his mind, how to get off that island was something else. For him it seemed an impossibility. He cried for help, barking and charging frantically up and down the island in sight of people on the path. His efforts must have paid off, for the next day the island's households returned to their usual family spats.

The second dog, unlike the first, seemed to limit the value and use of water to drinking. His owner, a very determined young man, had met his match. Both stood on the park's dock. The dog, with his feet firmly planted, and leaning away from the edge of the dock stubbornly refused to be coaxed, cajoled, pushed, or persuaded that he, a black lab, was a water dog, His "master" shouted, sweet-talked, danced about, threw sticks into the water, and in between his frustrated vocal efforts, looked over at the path, at the other people on the dock, held his arms out, palms up in an "I give up" gesture, and then went right back to his song and dance routine. The dog refused to be fooled or tricked into having a bath or performing as a retriever. Finally he just sat down and would not budge. The stand-off was a reminder of one author's comment.

"I've seen a look in dog's eyes, a quickly vanishing look of amazed contempt, and I am convinced that basically dogs think humans are nuts." 38

After such a performance - and perhaps there have been similar ones over time, with other friends, it's a wonder that people and dogs feel up to going for walks or romps around the park at any time. It turns out that no dog-person drama played out will deter either creature breed from taking each other for a walk, run, or stroll in the park.
Various approaches are demonstrated to navigate paths around the park, deep inhaling, exhaling, ventilating, irrigating, and defecating.

That leads to the question, "What's the best breed of dog one should buy and train, if the soul purpose is to enjoy trips around the park?"

Rather than first seeking a consultant for advice, a good look at what's already going on with dogs and owners in motion might clarify things. So what do we see happening over time?

A jogger running beside a dog that thinks it's a Greyhound. A jogger that thinks he's the Greyhound.
A man on a bike with a dog pulling the bike. A dog in a basket, licking the man's face. An in-line skater being pulled

by a dog. The dog heading for the trees. Dogs that lag behind, others that run ahead.

Dogs preoccupied with the joyful activity of courting, totally oblivious to their owners' embarrassment.

The dog who lifts his leg to pee on a tree, and falls down. The dog who squats, and the owner, with a bag from the park poop dispenser, who looks around as if it wasn't happening.

With all that happens when people and dogs seek the great outdoors, it might be helpful if instructions for participants were available to augment the signage that refers to park hygienics.

The instructions might, of course, take into account the incredible number of breeds that emanate from the Adam and Eve of the dog world- and if bird watchers have a legitimate right to practice their craft, so also might there be, dog watchers. There certainly is a good supply of breeds to engage in dog spotting, as there is for bird spotting. Perhaps as with annual bird counts, there could be dog counts.

Already in one month an avid dog fan spotted: three bassets, two sheep dogs, one collie, a dozen different dogs of oriental ancestry, one Scotty dog, a British bulldog, three tiny terriers, one grown up dog suitable for putting in one's pocket, a little dog with legs moving a mile a minute even when picked up, and a sausage hound. Wow! Just think if a day was set for a dog count, and it was given good publicity. The event might turn into a fantastic impromptu dog show.

One dog watcher couldn't help but be left with one haunting question to worry over when watching dogs and their owners take each other for walks. Do dog and owner personalities blend as the years pass in their relationship - or do owners choose dogs that match their own personalities?

There certainly are unique dogs, as there are unique

people, finding the park a place to enjoy: the little mother dog, and her two gangly, monster children. A dog looking like a rug who charges around as if he could see through a mass of hair, a little amputee dog scurrying down a path on three legs looking totally unaware of his handicap, and a sophisticated poodle who looked like it just stepped out of a beauty salon. There was a muzzled dog, and a Great Dane, taking its petite young owner for a run, a dog that prompted the woman to shout over her shoulder as she flew past,
"He's only a puppy, you know."

"I have a dog of Blenheim birth, With fine long ears and full of mirth; And sometimes, running o'er the plain, He tumbles on his nose: But quickly jumping up again, Like lightning on he goes!" [39]

Most folks with dogs who frequent the park have stories they could tell about how their, or others pets, show great tolerance and patience when dealing with their owners.
Some people amuse themselves by showing off their dogs intelligence by having them perform tricks such as seen on TV talk shows.
Some will absentmindedly scratch their dogs bellies and watch their pets legs twitch. Others have given their pets challenging foods to chew, even peanut butter that sticks to the roof of their pets mouths. Dogs with fleas have had funnels placed over their heads to prevent them scratching. Then there are the baths in the tubs where dog toe nails just can't gain a footing no matter how much they scramble to avoid splaying out, helpless under the application of brush and soap and towel rub down.
Someone once made a proposal, saying,
"Just as a child might be a mayor, or school principal for the day, how would it be if a person might be honoured by being a pet dog for a day?"
That of course won't happen, no one would voluntarily suffer the indignation that would go along with such a thing.

Yet dogs do, and despite it all, they remain loyal, and, more than that, we know they'll give their all, even, if need be, their lives to protect their masters.

"Even the tiniest poodle is lionhearted, ready to do anything to defend home, master, and mistress." [40]

"Dogs have given us their absolute all. We are the center of their universe, we are the focus of their love and faith and trust. They serve us in return for scraps. It is without a doubt the best deal man has ever made." [41]

14

The Other Creatures

Coarse concrete, shattering noises, acrid air, growling engines, and screeching brakes without, confined space, maddening irritations clawing at one's nerves within apartments, lodges, and housing units, force cooped up persons to find an escape to an unblemished space.

Aboriginal people who have known the freedom of breathing clean air, away from wind tunnel dusty grit, sanding face and hand, know and show by their appearance in Goose Island Park that all is good here. Like them, the city and town folk also can't help but gain a sense of well being in an environment where, biologically, they were meant to be. The truth is told by one who said,

"I am a part of all you see in Nature: part of all you feel: I am the impact of the bee upon the blossom; in the tree I am the sap that shall reveal the leaf, the bloom that flows and flutes up from the darkness through its roots." [42]

"All who feel deeply the life of the park will know that they must respond to the call of the park to return. All who deeply engross themselves in what they feel they must have to perform in human endeavours will know that all is for naught unless that which they pursue, sleep, riches, and health, to be truly enjoyed, must be interrupted." 43

Two heading in a big hurry along the park road, intent on getting back to dive into their office cubicle, had a second thought. They pulled over, parked, and talked their way over to a park bench facing the water. They sat, shifted around on the bench, and glanced around as if in some foreign place. Both, shifting their heads about, saw two suited figures lounging on the grass under the shade of a tired, scarred old tree. One on the park bench, said,

"Those two look like they are planning to be there all afternoon. How can they spare the time? I recognize that one. He's got a corner office."

"You do? Well, maybe he's heard what Ernest Hemingway once wrote."

"What?"

"I still need more healthy rest in order to work at my best. My health is the main capital I have and I want to administer it intelligently." 44

Park bench sitters, like the two suited and seated, gained membership in the unofficial park sitting club that took the time to soak up nature's perfume and appearance. Bench membership wasn't limited only to the "haves." Have nots belonged, too, because membership was as free as the air in the park.

This made some folks uneasy, especially lone walkers and joggers setting out early in the morning or late in the evening to do the rounds.

More than once, in different park settings, a homeless soul found the park his living room, the bench his couch for the night, and the washroom nearby his convenience, and, sometimes, his shelter from the rain or snow.

Sometimes in the shadows, a walker or jogger would pass a bench where two seated figures in ragged, soiled garb, would lean out as if to touch or beg, leaving the passing path users feeling uneasy or intimidated.

"One might speak to great length of the three corners of reality: what was seen, what was thought to be seen, and what was thought ought to be seen." 45

The metal crashing noise of the big army-green park refuse bins in clanking shut, gave notice of the presence of park frequenters of four kinds: the city maintenance worker, the responsible picnicker or dog owner, and the "bottle and can collector." Those who come across anyone or more of the first three take little notice of the approaches used to tackling the bin's lids. But the guy with the garbage bag, or bike with a basket, maybe towing a wagon, with dog for company, turns heads. The scavaging soul poking about in the "garbage" is another source of uneasiness or embarrassment for the comfortable, augmenting their life style with self care behaviour, followed by a second cup of coffee, or breakfast with a friend.

Conversation sometimes even included talk about others alleged behaviour. "How many more of those creepy characters will we see roaming the city, and the parks?"
"Who are you talking about now?
"You know, those who cash in their cans and bottles at the depot, visit the liquor store, then end up staggering about the streets stoned drunk."

One person among the coffee drinkers shared his uneasiness with what had been asked and assumed. He reminded the hard nosed person that one shouldn't jump to conclusions about the strange among the familiar. He quoted from an item titled "Rag-&-Bone Men" written by a person of the Jewish faith.

"The sheeny you can see frequenting the lanes, and uttering raucous cries of 'rags, bones, and bottles...' They are usually dressed in clothing that was made for somebody else, and are adorned...with whiskers..Little hunched-backed cigarette smoking men. It didn't matter to the peddlers (the rag and bone men) that some thought their line of work was one step above charity. Many a factory owner, shopkeeper, or scrap dealer began as a peddler and many a family survived on a peddler's income. This was a source of pride and self-respect that far outweighed any results. Their overriding goal was "to make it" in the new world because that meant security and assurance of a better life." [46, 47]

The coffee drinking question-poser turned to the Beaver magazine reader, and in response to this quote yawned, shifted the waist band of his expensive sweat suit, and said,
"Okay, but what's that got to do with anything."

The contents of the bags carried by the men who poke around in park garbage bins is no mystery. But green garbage bag carriers who hang around the docks and bouldered lake shore do rouse the curiosity of onlookers, especially when bags appear to be lumpy and very heavy.

One early morning when few people were about in the park, an early bird watcher did see a lakeshore lurker looking very suspicious. What was in his bag? Putting two and two together, geese sleeping on the grass, and others nearby in the water, and the lumpy bag, could it just be, that dinner was in the bag?

The onlooker never asked. He didn't want to get involved, just in case.

When the sun rose from its sleep, warming the winds, people appeared. Families drove up. Others stepped off city buses. Some biked in - all heading for the picnic shelters and tables. Kids began playing on the dock and on the rocks. So another day began with these purposeful people of all sizes, shapes, and ages joining the path walkers, joggers, and runners, in-line skaters, and strollers, the visually impaired, runners for a cause, adolescents, and lovers smooching on the little bridges and paths, elderly couples arm in arm; and loungers throughout the park, under shading trees, and on soft grass. Some wheel-chaired folk shared the spaces with disadvantaged joined by care workers and friends.

There they all were, alone, in groups, pairs, families blended or not, wearing whatever, heeding no dress code, nor limits on movement. They freely nodded in passing or mingled, except when cameras flashed, and wedding parties gathered to pose or witness the tying of knot, distracting them from their play.

Apart from the little annoyances of walkers, four abreast, hesitating to yield to passers, the odd bike rider or skater coming up from behind without warning, a few kids scurrying about keeping grown-ups on their toes - all in the park seemed to be at peace with the world, members of nature's extended family.

It's been said, "The family is one of nature's masterpieces." [48]

Sometimes kids did appear - roaming the park unaccompanied by grown-ups, but mingling with them. With their presence, a level of adult tolerance prevailed. For they seemed to recognize the truth that,

"If a child is to keep his inborn sense of wonder, he needs the companionship of at least one adult who can share it, rediscovering with him the joy, excitement and mystery of the world we live in." [49]

Though all these park pedestrians, with feet on the ground, prevailed in staking their claim on Goose Island Park, they tolerated riders with feet on the pedals. Parents, wobbling kids, seniors, youth, and serious racers or dirt bikers kept the slower of foot on their toes. The riders sported helmets, sweats, some even wore pant clips. Their bikes sported mirrors, bells, bike pumps and water bottles.

The regulars, like curling skips learning the lay of the ice, discovered the path's subtle hills and dips. Some even timed their movements to avoid the drenching from park lawn sprinklers that ambushed the unsuspected.

One could imagine the park whispering to riders, "Stay alert and aware." For the challenge included swerving and weaving around walkers and trees lining paths, surprising the startled who responded to that tail-gating by jumping aside, wheeling around or refusing to yield. Not only have refusals to yield impeded the progress of riders, but also concrete curbs have caused a few unsuspected riders to become airborne, having felt their whirling bike tires strike curbs.

Rising painfully from bleeding knees, torn and imbedded with grit, a shocked rider with painful ribs and elbows glances around teary-eyed and red faced. A mother and child, having just dodged the rider before he flew over the handle bars, watched the rider's dismal performance. The child, still grasping her mother's hand, looked up and asked, if that man did that on purpose.

Her mother, at loss for words, but not wanting to upset her daughter, blurted out,

"Well, yes, kind of, he's a bike park patrol person." The child, staring at the rider, limping down the path, said:

"But, does he have to do that to do his job good?"
Not quite knowing how to answer, nor knowing why she told her daughter a fib about there being such a thing as a park bike patroller, the mother said,

"Never mind, I'll tell you some other time. Let's catch up to grampa. I think that's him now to take us out for a burger. Isn't he nice, he's just come in from the farm."

"But, but... what about that man with the hurt knee and bike wheel?"

Picking up her concerned child, mumbling another "Never

mind," the mother ran towards her father, no doubt thinking, being an old and wise farmer, concerned about "all God's creatures." he'd know how to answer.

15

It Can Go Either Way

Sometimes persons in the park got hooked into conversation where the big questions of life were explored. The park gives people the opportunity to stop and reflect on what life is really all about - leading to the gaining of meaningful, useful insights.

Some might say the chief reason for doing things is to relieve boredom and that's all there really is. Others might say, No, it's to satisfy one's appetites or to be entertained.

One book in the Bible, Ecclesiastes (3:1-15) presents a ho hum attitude about life, suggesting life is really a futile chore where one is obliged to get through it as best one can, given there are many experiences one can't avoid. That blissful, fatalistic way may cause a disconnect with nature, and its potential to deliver surprises both good and bad.

An incident happened in an Arctic community where a young father and son left their home to walk parallel to the shore on a freezing winter day. The father had either missed hearing the weather report of an impending storm or ignored it. When they started out the sun was shining and visibility was good. A raging storm did develop with a strong wind blowing towards the shore, pushing the father and son from their sides. The father used that wind as a guide. Unfortunately, the wind changed to the opposite direction without the father realizing it. Consequently he, with his son, instead of hugging the shore as he thought he was doing, walked further away from safety onto the vast sea ice. Their bodies were found huddled together with the father's parka wrapped around his son.

In a book titled " Once Upon a LittleTown " by MacDonald Coleman there is a chapter called, "The Crazy Fisherman." In it the reader hears a youngster talking to Mr. Orchard who says;

"Everyone knows that Ben Orchard was slightly crazy, loony in the old beano." But, after reading the chapter, one wonders, was he really? For in the conversation Ben Orchard poses that profound perennial question that haunts us all,

" What are you living for?" The conversation goes on where old Ben suggests an answer. The story continues, ending with an interesting surprise. For the youngster who watches old Ben fishing, where even he, a youngster, knows there are no fish, hears Ben say finally, when challenged with that fact,

"Look Kid, I'll show you something. Look at my fishing rod. For a fishless creek you should always use a fishless fishing rod. "

Then the kid says,

" But you'll never catch a fish. "

" Yes I will. Anyway I'm a vegetarian and I don't eat fish. But yes I catch fish here. I caught you this afternoon and you've been a very pleasant nice fish.

Come and see me any time you like."

16

The Canoe

"There, stop there. No, its the next one. That's not it. Just go past that car, three down. See that parking space. It's across from the sign," he said.

"Where do you see a GARAGE SALE sign? I don't," she replied.

"It's just by that tree, " he shouted.

"Which tree?

"That tall one!"

"There's two tall ones. "

"The fattest one."

"They're both fat."

"That's true, but some are fatter at different parts of their bodies as you go up their trunk," he said.

"I don't see a trunk on either of those two."

"Which two?" He blurted back.

"The ones we've been talking about."

"I haven't been talking about trees. It's the sign, the Garage Sale sign we're looking for. Oh, heck, let's cross the road and see." He grew impatient.

"You go, I'll stay in the car. Wave, if there's anything worth looking at," she said.

"What are you looking for. I don't know what you want."

"You do so know what I look for at garage sales. You've seen me buy enough stuff."

"I haven't," he said, frowning.

"Well, what do you call that stuff on the back seat?

"Clothes."

"Right. So you do know what I look for," she said.

"Oh, this is silly." He looked across the street.

"What is, you telling me, I'm silly?"

"Oh, forget it. Let's go home. Pull out," he whispered.

"Okay, let's, I've only gone along with you this Saturday, because you wanted to buy. What was it you wanted to buy?" she asked, while digging around in her purse.

He shook his head. "I've had it up to here. That's it. Enough! Let's go."

She pursed her lips, then, "Hold on. Might as well find out what they've got here, since we're here already."

"Thought you said you didn't want to," he pouted. "Come on, let's go then."

"All right, but I'm not crossing over here. We'll go to the corner and cross, " she said firmly.

"Come on. Lock the car door. We'll cross over. The house is right in front of us," he shook his head.

" I'm going to the corner, and cross there."

"Suit yourself, I'll meet you here," he said.

"No, wait for me. Don't you want me with you?"

"Sure, but, let's go! I'll meet you on the corner on the other side, when you cross."

"If you're going to do that, why don't you just come with me to the corner and we'll cross together?"

"All right, but wait a minute. I'll cross over here, and just check to see if the sign says that it's today, and not yesterday."

"But if you do that, we won't be crossing over together," she said.

"Yes, but no sense both of us going to check. What if it

was yesterday?"

"Oh, have it your own way, I'll cross over right from here with you. I won't go to the corner."

He looked puzzled. "But if we do that, and both of us are killed, who will drive the car home?"

"Oh, come on. Let's go see what's there. Gosh, you're a darn fool, really!" she laughed.

As they crossed, "Wait, let those cars pass. Watch it. Gee, I didn't see that one. Where did it come from?"

"I don't know. Come on, hurry! Grab my hand. "

"I don't want to be on that side. We always walk with me on your left. "

He shouted, "Grab my hand. I wanted to be between you and the oncoming cars. That way, I'll get hit. In that way I'll have saved you."

"Yes but, when we get half way across, the traffic will be approaching us from the other side. Then what?"

"Then we'll switch sides. I'll get between you and the oncoming cars again," he shouted.

"Well, let's not just stand here in the middle of the road. Let's get moving before we're hit, all right!

"Okay, but..," he mumbled.

"Watch your step on the curb." She looked down, then at him.

"Now where is that ruddy sign?

"There, it is. It hasn't moved an inch since I last pointed it out to you," she said.

"I guess not. And it is today. Back alley. Say, I like those flowers. Do you think we could come back when they go to seed. You don't have any of those in your garden."

"My garden? It's yours too," she said.

"Then how come..."

"Forget it, let's see what they've got," she responded. "And don't haggle, least not while I'm close by."

"Why not, are you ashamed of me or something? I know I embarrass you in public," he said.

"That's not it. You just..."

"Well, if that's the way you feel, I'm going back to the car," he whined.

"No, come on now. You look and I'll look."

"All right, but if there's no prices on things, can I ask, maybe dicker a bit?" he asked. Then knowing the answer, "Come on, I'll find you some books."

"You read, too," she said. "You find your books. I'll look for mine."

"But I know the kind of books you like too," he said, lifting his chin.

"Okay, name some authors that I like."

"I forget," he said, tucking his chin into his neck.

"See, you don't know, and for goodness sake stop it. You're drawing a crowd."

"What do you mean, drawing a crowd!" He shouted.

"Lower your voice, will you, I didn't come here to have you put on a performance."

"Who is? Not me! Say what's that over there. My gosh, it is, a canoe! "

"Think you could get it home?" she said.

"I don't even know if I want it. Whole bunch of things I've got to consider." he said.

"Like what?"

"Like, you know."

"No, I don't know. You tell me," she said.

"Forget it, I'll ask how much it is." He looked around.

"And..?"

Turning back to her, "Say, do you see who is doing the selling?"

"And..? Tell me what else do you have to consider, finding out about.

"How am I'm going to get it home," he mumbled, "that's if we decide to buy it. Maybe it's sold already."

"Maybe it is," she said.

"If it is, how come it doesn't have a sold tag on it?"

"Maybe, it's sold, just the same," she replied.
She patted him on the shoulder."Why don't you ask? You're the one who wants it."

"How do you know that?" He stared at her.

"You're interested in it aren't you."

"Shoo. Not so loud! The guy, he'll have the upper hand, if I want to dicker," he whispered.

"Are you going to?"

Looking down at his feet, "I don't know. Should I?"

"Should you what?

"Dicker, or ask the price? Maybe both," he said, smoothing the canoe's skin.

"Good gosh, why don't you go and ask him. He's over there. See? "She sounded frustrated.

"I will, I will, don't rush me. Got to look it over first." He looked up and down its fifteen feet.

"Thought you had."

"I did, but I'm still not sure. It's a lot of money."

"How do you know. There isn't even a price tag on it. " Her voice sounded impatient.

"Well, it's bound to be."

"Maybe not," she countered.

"Maybe so," he said.

"Oh, go and ask. You might be surprised."

"Let me just look at it some more."

"Yeah, you do that - and the owner will know for sure that you're really interested! I can just see the price going up sky high right now."

"How do you know that. He wouldn't be that kind of guy."

She looked exasperated. "Oh, for goodness sake, I'll go and ask. You keep looking."

"No, I'll go, I'll go. Do you think it's still for sale. Do you think the price is right?"

She shook her head, "I thought all that you were worried

about was how you are going to get it home."

"I was, I am. But first I've got to find out something."

"You mean, the price?"

" No, whether it leaks or not."

"What about the price?" she asked.

"I won't have to ask him that, if he tells me it leaks."

She said, " He wouldn't sell it, if it leaked. Besides, that would make it cheaper."

"He most likely inflated the price too much to start with, knowing I'd try to dicker him down."

"Look, you haven't even really talked to the guy yet. How do you know what he's like, and whether he'd play that game?" she asked.

"I'm a pretty good judge of character."

"What, you can tell, just by looking at him from over here?"

He quickly glanced around. " Don't stare at him. He might think that we're talking about him."

"Well, we are!"

"Yes, but not about him - about his canoe."

"How does he know that?"

He tossed his head back, "He doesn't. But I do."

"Look, what's the problem with you. If you don't want to go any further with this, and you don't want me to talk to him for you, and you don't want to talk to him yourself - well, then let's get out of here, and go home." She started for the gate.

"But I do, at least I think I do." he mumbled.

"Okay then, let's find out what he's asking for his canoe, for goodness sake! Come with me."

The two stood by the man wearing a carpenter apron. They waited till he'd finished talking to a man holding some tools in one hand, a cell phone in the other.

"Hi, is your canoe still for sale," she asked.

"Yes."

"How much are you asking?"

"Two hundred."

"Does that include the paddles and life jackets I see there," he asked, holding back his eagerness.

"No. They're extra."

"How much total? "

"Two-twenty five."

"Would you take two hundred for the lot, canoe and everything there?" he asked.

"I don't know, I wouldn't think so. Hold on, I'll ask my mom. It was my dad's canoe. "

The aproned man returned, the screen door slamming behind him.

"She said, If you want the thing that badly, take it! Two and a quarter for the lot, two paddles, two life jackets, and that rope there. The paddles are new."

"Well, thanks anyway." He smiled. "Oh, by the way, does your canoe leak?"

"No."

"All right, two hundred for all of it," he said, looking so serious. Then, "Canoe too?"

"Huh?"

"It's a deal. Will you take a cheque?"

"I don't know about that."

"How about this. I'll go to the bank and get the money. If you haven't sold it when I get back, I might buy it."

"That's fine. Excuse me, I've got to talk to the person over there. I think that he wants to buy something."

She gave him a poke in his ribs with her elbow.
"You said to the man you would."

"Yeah, I will, If it's still here, that is. Since our car won't do to get it over to our house, he'd have to help me out with that. If he can, then I guess it's a deal."

"And if he can't, " she asked, "then what are you going to do then?"

"I guess a canoe sitting over here won't be much good to me."

"Meaning?"

"Well, I guess I won't buy it."

"But you said, 'It's a deal.'" She looked angry.

"I know, but we didn't shake hands on it."

The man in the apron returned, and smiled faintly, "Look, I'm sorry, but please, you two decide what you want to do?"

"My wife and I have to discuss it a little more. We'll get back to you, okay?"

"That's fine, I'll be over there," shrugged the apron man.

"Now look. See, you've got that guy mad."

"So what? That's his problem," he said.

"You must admit, you haven't really made his day. You know, I think I've had enough, let's go home."

"No," sounding anxious. " Let's go get the money."

"Why, you don't seem to want to buy the darn thing," she said.

"I'm thinking about."

"Well, think about it in the car!"

They started back from the bank.

"Okay, you got the money. Now, do you want to go and see if it's still there?"

"Yeah, sure. Do you think he'd take two hundred if we pay cash?" He gave her a light tap on her hand.

"You're going to embarrass me. When we get back there, I'll wait in the car."

"We don't even know if it will still be there, and even if it is, we don't know whether it will be sold or not."

"Well, darn it. Find out," she groaned.

He drove down a street that looked familiar while they searched for the house with the Garage Sale sign.

"Where's the house again? Are we on the right street?" he asked.

"You don't think it's moved do you?"

"I think it's that one. Or is it that one?" He looked bewildered. "Can't see the sign. Is it by or behind the tree?"

She sighed, "Which tree, there's two of them close together."

He eyed the row of cars to his right. "I'll park the car first."

"What about there, between those two. It's a big enough space."

"Not there. I'll drive up a bit. Don't want to get bumped from behind by not giving the driver of that car the room to pull out if he's finished shopping before we are."

"How do you know if it's a him? It could be a her."

"What are you talking about?"

"The driver in the car behind the car that you were going to park in front of."

"You mean the one that we can't see."

"Yes, that one."

"Oh, forget it, I'll park here. Let's get it over with."

"You going to go to the corner to cross over?"

"No, I'm going to cross here with you - taking the short cut like we did before."

He said, "Maybe, we'd better not do it that way. No sense both us getting killed by a car. Better you go to the corner and cross. I'll risk crossing here, and if I get killed, then you can inherit the canoe."

"I don't want the darn thing!"

"Then give it to someone else."

"Who?"

"I don't know!"

"Maybe we shouldn't buy it, till we decide who should get it when I go," he said.

"What do you mean 'go.' If you're thinking what I'm thinking, I'll go before you do. I'm just about ready to have a heart attack, or something worse right now. Enough!"

"You said that before," he smiled.

"What? "

"Enough."

"Come on. I'm exhausted. Watch the curb when you get across the road here. You almost tripped on it the last time." She led the way.

"That's sure a narrow walk to the back beside the house here. Look, there's those nice flowers. I've got to remember the house and street number so we can come back in the fall, like I said, to get some of those seed pods." He leaned down to touch the plants.

"Why in heaven, do you want them. You're not the gardener."

" I know, but I like looking at the results of your good work."

"Enough!"

"Enough, you said it again."

"Oh, shut up!"

When they got to the back of the house, the crowd had thinned out. The man with the apron came over to greet them. "Well, it's still here."

"Is it still for sale? Same price, with all the stuff thrown in?" he asked, trying to look non-committal."

" Yes, sure."

"Got a way to get it over to my house?"

"Think so."

"You take a cheque?"

"What?"

"Just joking."

"Give me your address. I'll get my brother-in-law to help me. He's got a truck."

"Phone me first, make sure we're home before you deliver it. Here's the money, two hundred. For all, right? And you're sure it doesn't leak. Oh, and I'll need a receipt. Mark it 'Paid in Full.'" He sounded so authoritative.

"Just wait, I'll go in the house and get my book. In the meantime feel free to look around. You might find some more bargains."

"I will."

She said, " Give me a few minutes, I didn't get a chance to see if there is anything here that I'd like."

He, too, was still looking. "Hey, gee, I didn't notice that set of snow tires over there by the fence. They look like new."

"Maybe they leak," she said. "Just don't even think about it! Here comes your man now with your receipt."

She turned to the aproned man and said, "My husband and I are on our way now. Thanks again."

"But..." her partner stuttered.

" Never you mind!" she said, grabbing his arm.

Time passed. The two were standing outside looking over at the turned over canoe.

"Gosh, it's been a week since we got it home from the garage sale. How am I going to get it to Goose Island Park Lake? Roof rack, and straps. CanadianTire will have them. I'll put it on top of the car. What do you think?"

She said, "I just don't understand you. Why didn't you figure that out before you got the canoe."

"It was a good deal. Couldn't pass that up." He looked so sincere.

"All right, you've got your good deal, now what?"

"Now." he said. "I'll get it all set up, slide it onto the roof rack, and strap it down. Nothing to it!"

"Right, I'll believe it when I see it."

"Believe it!"

After coming back with the equipment that he needed, he fussed about in preparing for the big moment.

"Okay," she said, "Now let's see you load it!"

With his hands on his hips he said, " Brings back memories of when I portaged canoes."

"You were younger then, and stronger."
"I can still do it. Just need to get it onto my shoulders." He flexed his muscles and pressed his body into action.

"Watch it, you're going to hurt yourself."
"No, I'll be okay. I'll just load it from the side of the car here," he said, most reassuringly.
"You won't."
"Yes, I will, just got to tip the side up, then flip it over onto its back."
She looked doubtful. " Which side is the back; the part that goes in the water, or the open part that you sit in?"
"I won't sit. Most of the time I'll kneel."
Looking concerned, she said, " Like now. If you don't give up on trying to do it that way, you'll be kneeling all right, then flat on your face. Don't be so stubborn. That way won't work!"

"Stop talking. Can't you see, my knees are shaking. I'm in distress... Now see what you made me do! I almost made a huge scratch on the car."
" Why don't you try it another way?"
"I will. Just give me another minute to think... Got it! Back the car up. Turn it around. Back it up again so the rear of the car is pointing to the front of the canoe."
" What do you mean?" She looked confused and doubtful.
"Please, just get in the car. I'll direct you. Just watch my arm movement. Open your window so you can hear me." He patted her on the shoulder.

"I'll try. But don't blame me if I crunch your ruddy canoe from the back."
"I won't. Just do what I tell you. It'll be okay."
"Hope so," she mumbled under her breath.

She got the car into position, put it in reverse, and began.

"STOP!" Okay, a little further. NO, NO! Go forward again. Now try, Back...Back...Back. Whoa."

She shouted, "It won't work. It won't work, I can't do it. You back it up. I quit!"

"I didn't fire you. Ah, come on back. Tell you what. I'll pull the canoe up to the back of the car, get under it, lift it up, and, once I get the front end onto the rack, I'll hoist it up, and slide it onto the car rack from the back here. You don't have to do anything, other than watch it doesn't slide off the rack from the side."

"You and that canoe. I wish you'd never bought it. You'll look like part of a turtle when you get under it - and, then what if it does decide to slide off the top, falling to the side. What do you want me to do about it then? Catch it?"

"No, do what I'd do," he laughed.

"What?"

"SWEAR! "

"You're a big help," she shouted,

The drama continued.

"Well, here it goes, under, lift, slide. Hey, it's on. We did it."

"You did it. But haven't you forgot something?"

"What?"

"The straps."

"Where are they?"

"In the trunk."

"So?" he shouted.

"How you going to lift the trunk lid, without the canoe nose-diving off the front of the car?"

Exasperated, he shouted. "Why didn't you remind me about that before? I just about broke my back getting the thing on top."

"You know why. You didn't ask."

He was just about ready to try to get the canoe off the car top, when he found that he was able to slide the canoe forward on the rack just enough to lift the trunk lid slightly, reach in, search around with his hands, and dig the straps out of the trunk. Apart from some wicked looking scratches on his wrists and arm, he came out of the searching effort fairly unscathed.

He went back to securing the canoe to the car. "Can't just leave it unstrapped. Here I go again. Once more, lift, and walk the blessed thing onto the car top. Wish the heck I didn't buy the darn thing. "

"You said it. I didn't. Now it's up there and strapped down, how are you going to get it off and into the water at the park?"

"I'll think of something. Do you have any ideas."

"Let's get it there. Maybe someone can help you offload it," she said, looking very weary.

"No way! I'll do it myself. I'll think of something."

"You said that before."

"Come on," he said, "let's go. You drive. I'll watch to make sure it doesn't slip off before we get there."

" What do you think it's going to do, shake itself off, like a dog shakes off water after a swim. Oh, heck, let's go."

She drove very slowly down the road circling the park. The canoe bounced and squirmed on top of the roof rack, tensing the straps taut. But they held.

Breathing a sigh of relief, the two arrived. Stepping out of the car, they began to size up the situation.

"Now, we're here. Now what?"

"See the boat ramp there. Back down it a bit, enough so when I get it off, I won't have to drag it too far before sliding it down the ramp."

"You're kidding of course," she said in astonishment.

"No, you can do it. "

"I can't. You know!"

"You can!"

"I won't!"

"Okay," he says, "change places. I'll do it! Gee,

it's always the same."

Not happy with that remark, she said, "What do you mean by that?"

"Never mind, forget it."

"No, I won't forget it. Just what do you mean!"

"You know, when ever... Oh, drop it."

"No, I won't drop it. You tell me what you mean!" she persists. "You tell me what you mean, or I'll go home right now."

"Let me get the canoe off first."

"Then what are you going to do. How are you going to get it home after you do your canoe on the lake thing?"

"I don't know, never thought about that."

Coming to his rescue she says, "Okay, tell you what we're going to do. We have two choices. One, you tell me how long you want to paddle about, and I'll come back and get you and the canoe. Or two, I'll wait here while you do your thing."

Uncertain, he asks, "What do you want to do?"

"You decide, it was your decision to start this whole affair."

"You mean, we're having an affair?" he asked.

" You know what I mean," she said.

"Yeah, our marriage up to now has been a lot of fun. Kind of like an affair," he laughed.

"That's fine. Now let's get on with what we've decided."

"What have we decided?"

"About what?" she asked.

"What you're going to do while I'm on the water?"

"So, decide!"

"No, you decide."

"It seems to me." she sighs, "we've been through this before."

"Okay, how would it be if we vote?"

"Huh? That's silly. Who would break the tie?"

"Let's ask that guy coming along there."
She asked, "Which one?"
He points, "The one with the two dogs."
"Maybe we could have them vote too," she laughed, "if we can just explain to them the pros and cons of the two options."

"Now that is ridiculous!" he says.
"That's right, she says, "I'll stay and wait for you to get the canoe in the water, paddle about, and load it back up after."
"Will you do that. You're a dear! "
"Now don't start again. Just get on with it."
"All right," he asks," where's the car keys?"
"You've got them. I gave them to you." she said.
"No, you didn't."
"I did, too. Search your pockets."
"I just did."
"Oh no, did you lock them in the car? " She gasped.
"No, I wouldn't do that. I always have them in my hand when I get out of the car."
"Well, check anyway. Can you see the ignition switch from the other side. Can you? Look see..."
By then he's struggling to keep his composure. "Don't rush me. Don't panic. No, they're not there."
"Thank goodness for that. Where can they be? Check your pockets again. No, on second thoughts, let me. What are these?"
"Keys. What would I ever do without you?"
"Never you mind. Do your thing."
"Okay, here we go. I'll back it up to the ramp. You tell me when to stop. Okay?" He tries to look confident.
"Okay."

It then began. A few people stopped on the path and stared.

"This is it then," he shouted. "Here we go. I'm backing up."

The car lurched, stalled then came to life again.

"Why did you stop? I didn't tell you to. Come on, a little more, a little more. There, you did it again."

"Did what?"

"Stopped before I told you to."

"Maybe that's far enough anyway. I'll try rolling it off from the side, " he shouted.

" You do that, and I'll scream for help if you get stuck with it in mid air."

"Well," he joked," say a prayer. Here it goes. I'm going for broke. Going, going-gone. Oh my God, did it hit anything? Did it break its back? It almost did mine."

"Never mind, you pulled it off so far. You can finish the job." She stepped back and surveyed the scene.

"I'm glad you've confidence in me," he said, "I'm not that sure of myself. Though, you've been with me through , thick and thin throughout the years. It's been great. You have propped me up so well."

"Sound's like you're giving me your last words on your death bed. Are you expecting the worst on the water or something?"

"No," he said. "It's just that I'm feeling a bit rusty."

"At doing what, dying?"

"No, it's just been quite awhile since I paddled my own canoe."

"You've been doing that all along, and very well too."

"I guess," he smiled, "We've not done too bad together."

"Now don't get too mushy, mushy. Not now."

"Later, maybe."

"Get on with it!"

"Okay," he said, taking her hand, "What are you going to do while I'm out there?"

"I'll walk around the park or something. I'll be here when you get back. Never fear."

"See you soon then. Shouldn't be too long. Once around the lake will do."

He walked down to the water's edge, pulling, and pointing the canoe's nose out into the water. He thought, when I get out there I'm going to have a view of things that few in the park experience.

"Here goes. No one is going to mind me talking to myself out there. Push it out, nose pointing away from the water's edge. Hop in. Too soon. Dragging the bottom. Could break the paddle shoving off. Maybe not. Wow. Better sit down. Legs are shaking. It could tip. Sit or kneel down you fool! Oh heck! Should have had the wider seat end near the shore line. Now, got to keep my centre of gravity low, get my legs over that stringer, and sit, or kneel. Now swing the canoe away from the shore. I don't know if I can do it. My gosh, surprised myself! It's turning around and away from the ramp.

Watch the bank there. Just missed it. Now, can I keep this thing going in a straight line. Seems if I paddle on one side and then on the other, it stays a bit straight. But each time I lean over to dip the paddle on that side or the other side, it gets tippy. Oh I remember now. Dip the paddle then feather it, sort of give it a twist with the wrist, and then pull it back. Hey, that seems to work. Now what?

Paddle! Watch it, you're going straight for the spewing water fountain. Paddle away. Look, you're getting soaked. Now watch it, that red dragon boat buoy is right in front of you. To the left, to the left! Left, not the right! Just made it by.

Now what. Keep close to the shore. You didn't put your life jacket on. Do it now. Good thinking. But it's at the front. Oh no! Can I get up there and not tip the ruddy thing over? Did it. Mission accomplished. Getting it and squirming into it wasn't too bad after all.

On we go. Sailing, sailing on the...how does that song go..?

Hey. Getting near the Japanese Garden shore-line. Be nice if I could pull in there - but where? Maybe another time.

Wind's picking up. I think I've got the hang of this paddling again. Just like when I was a teenager up north. Must look pretty competent moving fast over the water. Feeling a little proud.

Maybe, I can race those runners on the path by paddling parallel to them. Well anyway, I think I can keep up with the walkers. It was a nice idea at any rate.

Keeping company with those ducks and geese is something I wouldn't miss for the love of it. Oh heck, a gift from the air, just about got me on the shoulder. The splat should come off my knee. Lucky it wasn't a crow or raven egg coloured guck. Forget it. Look ahead, geese! Maybe I can get closer. Unsociable bunch, swimming away from me, mooning as they go. Impolite!

Now what, heavy going all of a sudden. Should have tried skirting this stuff. Weeds on the paddle, in the boat when I dip the paddle up and out. This is no good! Get out of here. Think those ducks over there must be laughing themselves silly, with me trying to pole out of this.

Finally out of it. Now, maybe I can put on a demonstration for those on the shore. No competition though. I'm the only person on this water. No one on the shore seems to be paying any attention to me. What is getting their attention. Oh, over there, a huge white pelican. He's putting on quite a show . A cool dude as a teen would say. What's that pelican got that I don't have? Silly question.

Now I'm under the bridge, getting close to the Island.

Think I'll try the side of the island that I couldn't see from the shore. Always been curious about what there is to see. That's a bit disappointing. Not much of anything to see on its banks.

Maybe when I swing to the right around the Island, I can stir up some geese or ducks to feel powerful when I startle them, and they take off. Here it goes. Darn, they're just ignoring me. Some squawking, but that's usual. No sense trying to stop and visit them. I know what they're up to, spring time and all. I don't think I'll do another around the lake. Knees hurting, arms hurting. I think even my feelings are hurt. Haven't really impressed anyone, neither the geese, nor even myself. I guess I'll head for the boat ramp, find my partner, and head for home.

Look, not even a soul to greet me when I paddled to shore. What was this all about, anyway. Did I miss something? Maybe, the whole business was a re-enactment of life?"

"Oh, there you are. How was your trip?"
"It was great!"

"May the roof above never fall in.
May we below, never fall out."
An Irish grace.

17

Nature's Farm

The park path felt the soft treading feet of so many farm and city folk, working and retired. Two grey-haired persons walked side by side, one, a widow of a teacher, the other a retired farmer's wife who had moved into the city. As they walked they shared. On one day, farm life came up in their conversation, in particular, the creatures, big and small that shared the outdoor environment, just as walkers did with creatures in the park.

The teacher's widow encouraged her walking partner to talk about what it was like back on the farm. Their walk was enriched that day, as the farm wife and mother relived and share her memories.

One experience followed another, and on and on, with little interruption from her walking partner who, fascinated by the telling, only responded with a smile, a laugh, or a brief pause to listen even more intently.

"I think every bug and moth and mosquito had passed by the farm, and some stayed much too long. I told some town friends, 'Be careful, I think they are heading west to see you folks.'"

"One summer, well, there was even more than one, we had hardly any rain. The grass needed a drink. It got so brown. It was then I'd cut cattails so low that they'd be under water. Then they didn't grow so easy again. I'd pull them out by the roots. It was always a problem in the pond. They would grow about 8 feet at least."

"As soon as my neighbour took his cattle out in the fall, I guessed I'd have to spray to kill them cats tails."

"Cats! Once I had one special black cat. A neighbour brought it down as his wife didn't like its mewing. It hadn't eaten for 3 days and was getting frail. It was a house cat but I just fed it at the barn and hoped it would stay around there. My neighbour said it was a Tom, but I told him the first batch of kittens was his problem."

"Racoons, now, they were something else! Once a racoon was on the rampage. He came through the yard and down my sidewalk one night. I couldn't believe how big he was. His legs were a good ten inches long and he had a big tail. He passed the house and headed up to the Quonset. That same night I closed the windows upstairs in case he decided to come in, as he would tear the screens. I had heard it on the roof on some other nights. We set the trap that night. I had a bucket of microwave popcorn and the butter in it smelled rancid. He should just love that. We caught it. Now what? My son wouldn't kill it, so I hoped to drown it, but he said he'd take it to the lake and drop it off. My husband tried that with the first racoon he caught. He took it to a lake miles away, and in 3 days, a very tired racoon came back and feasted on my chickens."

"One week the fellows were so excited. They said they saw a rat in the barn. After a lot of commotion and talk in the house to get a gun, they found it was just a muskrat. They wouldn't buy any hay from out of province because a rat maybe would be in the bale. So they were always on the look out for a rat or rattlesnake in the hay that came in."

"We did have deer in the yard, though. They disappeared during the daytime and came out at night. My son tried shining the flashlight on them and on the trees to shoo them away. But they just stayed. We worry about them chasing Rascal, the dog. He was such a snoop and often got into trouble."

"Deer, we could do without, but not our old horse. One night it dropped to -21, and with little breeze, it was really crisp out. Our horse was back on its feed. He had refused to eat for awhile and was really looking depressed. We decided something was wrong with his feed. I got a new bag of oats and had some molasses put in it. He really enjoyed that. My son brought some grass and alfalfa hay in and we started that and he likes that too. We think maybe the oats may have been stored near a pesticide, paint or diesel products at the supply store, and that's what turned him off. We don't know why he didn't like the first hay. Maybe a coon or coyote visited the bales."

"Still exciting days at the corral. Had a cow that was really protective and we had to get her out of the bunch with her calf. A helpful fellow was so tired of trying to move her. He told another man to take the deck and tractor in and drive up by her. He had a lariat. I was on the deck trailer of hay. I asked him what he intended to do. He said he was going to rope her. I asked him what he would do when he roped her, as I knew we couldn't handle that old cow. He would tie her to the tractor, and another man could drag her in.

Well, it was so funny to see him standing on a bale trying to rope that cow. She bobbed her head and scraped her front foot and snorted. A couple of spectators hoped he would miss - and he did. They tired of that game, but meanwhile the calf moved forward and the one man jumped off the deck, grabbed the calf and ran, the cow right on his heels. As long as he had the calf in his arms he was safe. All turned out well in the end."

"Some cows decided to have their calves. One remained on hold. She wanted another cow's new calf and just thought it was hers. She created such a fuss. All the others were stirred up. She just planted all four feet securely on the ground, looked us square in the eyes and bawled, and bawled. My husband said she should calve sometime in the night. We checked her many times, but no go, so we ate popcorn and apple sauce and at 3 a.m. gave up and went to bed. Our son checked in at 6 a.m. - still nothing doing. Later, the other son came over as the forecast was winds. He tagged the other calves and put them in the north coral far away from that still-expecting cow, and sure enough, then she decided to have her calf. She was so excited. And a little later all was quiet around the farm."

"We found a young calf in the pasture. Not good! He hadn't been getting any milk because his mom had mastitis in her udder. He was so thin he wouldn't have made a good sandwich. We brought them in and I fed him for 2 weeks on a bottle. Still he stayed thin for quite awhile, but in time, he got stronger. I called him Lucky."

"Often we had wet springs. Snow didn't stay long on the ground. It melted readily. Lots of calves ran and kicked about. We tried to encourage them to stay on drier pasture as the corrals were so wet. But calves had to come in to water.

"Calves needed lots of care. We were always glad when they had their shots for black leg because they were so susceptible in the hot weather."

"On at least one occasion, everybody was concerned about hoof and mouth. There was a meeting at the town hall with two veterinarians speaking. I felt like people were finding the worry stressful."

Less worrying was having birds about the farm.
"As with most springs so many birds came back. It was nice to hear them. I remember one day we heard a strange noise of tapping. We looked and looked and found a big woodpecker sitting on top of the metal casing of the electrical transformer high up on the pole. It was tapping on the metal, sending an SOS back home no doubt. That went on for quite awhile. I looked the picture of it up in the book and it said it was a Yellowhammer something."

"I looked forward to spring time. I think back to one early spring. The pond was free from ice. The geese were having a good swim, and the wind was tossing the waves high. A week before, the geese flew in, landed and slid a good 10 feet on the ice. It was good to have them back. Lots of owl activity, and plenty of hooting, but I didn't see any owls on the nest at that time."

"Another time, I remember the wind blew so hard the owls were walking. They were huddled together and weaved to and fro. After the wind died down they began flying and hooting again."

"Little birds had to watch out for those owls. A very little bird had a nest in the very little bird house in the tree. Some of the roof came off, and when I tried to straighten it, the bird looked out. She really needs air in there. So maybe that's why it was coming off. The female bird was a gentle brown and the male, a beautiful bright, canary yellow. Wouldn't you know it, the male got the best, but being a bright colour, maybe, the worst."

"I also remember once, we were putting the motors on the wheel movers. A meadowlark came to see what we were doing. It sang the most beautiful song. A time of spring."

"It wasn't long after that - that summer came along with its gifts. So many beautiful days. Birds chirped and burbled. The grass grew greener and higher. And the rain, we appreciated it, every drop. So much to take pictures of. Took some from last year to the photo shop in town. I forgot to keep the negatives. Maybe did that because there's nothing to really be negative about."

"I remembered also planting flowers and mowing, and mowing. Something else - Rascal, when he ran into a skunk. So we pickled him in vinegar -that was the second time. Needless to say, Rascal wasn't the most popular dog around the farm for some time. We said we'd have to trap that skunk, but hadn't much luck. It probably has young ones and just came out when the sun was saying good-bye for the day."

"Still, no matter what, can't say much bad about nature's farm. For even when the birds, skunks, creatures like Rascal, and others head for shelter, I always remembered- that in the wind and dust blowing, even a bad day of farming was a good day of living."

So, too, was it a good day of living that the two had shared that afternoon on the walk through the park.
Maybe, they'd do another walk sometime and talk about this business of getting old ... maybe.

Someone once said, to be any earthly good when one gets old, one needs to forget to remember. How so? Keeping one's head screwed on right, means paying attention to the here and now. True, useful wisdom for the young comes from sharing years lived,

"The more sand has escaped from the hourglass of our life, the clearer we should see through it." 50
True, also, that,
"Old wood best to burn, old wine to drink, old friends to trust, and old authors to read." 51
True, again that,
"Birds sing after a storm; why shouldn't people feel as free to delight in whatever remains to them?" 52

But, as demonstrated by many vigorous old-in-years, but not in body and mind, fast hoofing it down the park paths, and laughing and playing with children, no one need wallow in the waters of tepid philosophy. Rather, as the active in the park surely must believe,
"If you carry your childhood with you, you never become older." 53
And, "Age is an issue of mind over matter. If you don't mind, it doesn't matter." 54

Though they don't sing that theme out loud as convincing lyrics, many who are park regulars, say, "keep putting one foot in front of the other." head down, doggedly determined.
Perhaps they remember what Charles M. Schultz, author of the Peanut's cartoon once said, thinking there is no time to waste, life is precious,

"Just remember, once you're over the hill you begin to pick up speed."

Some others may have had the same thought, and so as

couples, breakfasted or lunched together, often parking their canes, or motorized wheelchairs within reaching distance.

Then there were others who frequented the park, looking very attentive, focused, and keenly interested, not in their personal well being so much, but rather on what was still out there for them to connect with and contribute to.

Somehow they seemed to latch on to the idea that for example,
"To be seventy years old is like climbing the Alps. You reach a snow-crowned summit, and see behind you the deep valley stretching miles and miles away, and before you other summits higher and whiter, which you may have strength to climb, or may not. Then you sit down and meditate and wonder which it will be." [55]

So the bystander, viewing the human activity, and being long-in-the -tooth himself, came to the conclusion that,

"A man is not old as long as he is seeking something." [56]

Sad to say though, he sees in the park evidence of where that note about appreciation of life is not heard even by some young in years, and the result is a disaster.

18

The Abandoned Clothes

Oh, that hurts. Gees, I don't want to get up, but I've got to uncurl those toes. What if I just relax. Start by bending my knees, then work my way down. Doesn't help. The warm blanket's better than cold when my feet hit the floor. What time is it? Darn, the clock slipped off the side table. Never went off. Right, I didn't set it. Amazing, I can see with the night light it's five. Oh, can't uncurl my toes. Got to sit up, stand up, push down. Forget the slippers. Bathroom first. It feels some better. Oh, its better now, Go back to bed. No, can't take a chance, better get up. Gees, now that bloody kink in my back. Can't be kidney stones. Feels like muscle spasm, maybe. Hate to turn the bathroom light on, always have to squeeze my eyes tight, then open them slowly. Better, I guess than a kink in my foot or toes. The message in the mirror doesn't help my disposition.

The Health watch on TV says sagging stomachs, the bloated look, not good for the heart. What time is it? Its not light yet. The exercise bike, that's a possibility. No, I said I'd start running around the park. Maybe the short way across the two bridges, and around that lagoon bit. I'll dress. Sweats, yes. This is different. Haven't felt so determined about "restoring my body." I remember I could get into those things in the closet. Should have given them to Sally Ann. Still think I could fit into those reminders of being in better shape.

    Well, soon it will be light. Don't want to wake anyone, though. Want to surprise them with the kettle on, toast smells when I get back. They'll be pleased I got out and did it. Where are those runners, the new ones, that they showed me how to slip the laces through loops at the top. I'll be just like those runners doing the lake path, and still able to talk when they run by, clopping along, gasping for breath types. But, like them, I'll get over that. Sit on the chair or the step to put them on. Big decision this early in the morning. Undo the laces more. A shoe horn doesn't seem the thing for these.

    Will I leave the light on above the stove? The only thing is it reminds me to get that builder to fix the fan. A bunch of things to do. I wish I hadn't signed off on this new house. I like the smell of new, but it's the little things. Just as bad a kinks in toes. It's light enough. I won't drive to the park. A couple of blocks to warm up. That will stretch the stiffness out. When I get by that long bit of chain fence keeping people off the golf course I'll pick up speed. It has seemed to cool down a bit, and the grass is wet. Better stay on the sidewalk and path. This is good. Better tummy breathe from the bottom of the lungs. Even better bottom, then top of lungs. Fill them up. More gas, energy. Nobody around. Something about this warm up bit, can get to feel empty, not just stomach, but the whole business. It's cleansing. Well, which way shall I go, the long way running by the golf course, or past the guns to my left, and swing around by the picnic shelters and washrooms. That's the way. Finish off with the long bit.

This is weird. I thought I'd meet someone by now. I look like a runner, dressed just so, but maybe tomorrow I'll run. Now I'll just walk it. Must be the first one out here. Well there's the floating docks, benches, pier, I'll keep going. No one in the parking lot. Not one car or truck. I must have beaten them all here. What's that over there, by the boat ramp, the space between the rocks. On the grass there. It's mounds, two of them. Thought at first they were a couple of ducks in the water. There are usually some around.

Clothes, what the..? Shoes, a pair; flannel shirt, faded jeans, ragged around the bottom, hole near the pocket, jacket, torn, greasy-like. Who'd leave those, all neatly piled. No under-shorts though. Why did I think of that. But the other lot, not tidied piled. Scattered pullover shirt, pants, out of style, no shoes, jacket near the path, all thrown about as if stripped off a body in a rush. A couple of bottles - not "This is Canadian " ones; bigger. Maybe whisky. Near the rocks. But this stuff must belong to two guys. No one in sight. Not on Goose Island, not in the water so calm, a bit sheltered between the lake rock lining, and the tree-sparse Island.

Oh my God! Gee I wish I had my cell phone. Got to get to one. Run! Got to get back to Lakeside Road. No, run. Wake up someone in the house across from the parking lot. Phone 911. I think they've drowned. Don't know who, but for sure that must have happened. But when I do that, will others come along, see the clothes, and do the same? Should I leave a note with the clothes. Ridiculous. Get going. Get going!

Shortly after finding the abandoned clothing, evidence of a tragedy, he sat on a park bench. His previous thoughts about nature's sensuality faded, replaced by the big questions of life - who are we, why are we here, and where are we going? He had often heard that death kicks us into gear to ask those questions. Now he was caught up in that tough struggle for answers. He began by remembering where he was, in the park, the home of other creatures like himself. That prompted another question. What makes humans, humans, and birds, and animals different?

People big and small passed by his park bench. He thought, Curious creature we are, herd animals. Once we had hair all over our bodies, that's why we get goose bumps. So we're something like all animals - same beginnings. Some high-falootin scientist he'd seen on TV's "Nature of Things' talked about culture being transmitted through genes, and one difference between other animals and humans was that humans have the power to direct evolution, whereas birds, and such have to go along with the changes.

He also thought about the question of nature or nurture, and which is which? Do some people's kids do the damnedest things because they were born bad, screwed up genes maybe, or did the grown-ups given to look after them, and the kids they hung around with have the greatest say about whether they'd be bad or good? One big difference between birds and animals and humans was that the other creatures, unlike humans, don't think about these things, they just do what comes naturally, and there just isn't good, or bad for them-there just is.
The thing about humans is,
"People see the world not as it is, but as they are." 57

Something else about humans, they have their own minds, and so not everyone sees things the same way, nor do they learn the same way-not like animals and birds. You take two or more people who size up a situation, or see an accident. Each sees it differently. Pondering over that idea, he asked himself, suppose a flock of geese flew over some humans in the park fussing over something that happened. Would each gander see things differently? And so on through the flock, each goose or gander sizing up what they saw, and concluding differently? Would they, on landing, debate who

is right and who is wrong? He didn't suppose so.
    Maybe that's one advantage humans have over birds, for, how does it go,

> "One point of view gives one a one dimensional world."
>
> 58

Humans have many points of view, and they sure let others know about them.
    The park bench sitter thought some more about this, and decided humans had a whole lot of other tendencies, some that even got them into a lot of trouble, or maybe worse, tied them in knots inside.
    Take young people for instance - from an older person's point of view, they get so hung up, as psychologists say, in preoccupations of youth, loneliness, resentment, anger, disillusionment,(now that's a big word!) self doubt, aimlessness, and so on...a few the same as nature's wild creatures.
    Maybe, he thought, young people could learn from a experiment where a big hungry fish was put into a fish tank. A glass partition halved the tank so on one side was the big fish, on the other side a juicy minnow. The big fish charged towards the little fish, only to bump his nose on the glass partition. He backed up, took another run at it, and bumped his nose again. Over and over he did this, but each time, he put a little less effort into it. Thinking, 'what the heck, it's impossible,' the big fish finally gave up! Then the partition was removed, and sadly the big fish starved to death.

    That whole idea about how people can get discouraged, rebuffed, and give up, seems to be something that the other creatures have in common.

    People, unlike the birds and animals though, he thought, had the power to get out of that trap. They, he included, had the power to decide which way they'd go in scratching their way through life. They could step out, risk, or, on the other hand retreat back into the womb, where it was warm, cozy, and safe, and do "nothing for nobody." Then again, they could decide whether they wanted to be pushed or pulled along through life, jump through hoops for others, have little control of their own lives, and end up being like puppets, with others pulling their strings, and 'jerking them around.' And when they were hurting inside, fed up with it all they'd go around grinning on the outside, and crying on the inside.

The bench sitter thought about a whole lot of other stuff that had to do with how he and others were built - that is, what makes humans tick. He thought about the business of mating - now that 's both a human and animal need. He thought about competitiveness - now that's a human thing. But he didn't think animals and birds were so caught up in that, except when food or the opposite sex was around.

Just then, a friend he often had coffee with came along, stopped, sat down, and away the two went on chewing the rag about people, why they do what they do, and what they should do, and don't do. They tossed question and answers about as if they catching ball.

"Why is it that when I start to pass someone, they speed up all of a sudden? It's as if they thought I wanted to challenge them to a drag race. That's damn silly, some of those I look over at as I pass, look like they're my grandparents, and I'm seventy-two."

"And what about the tail-gaters? You give them lots of time to pass on a four-laner, and they stay right up your backside. I haven't seen those geese in their formations acting that way. They seem to have more sense than that."

"Something else I noticed about some people. In fact I think it may be even one of my hang-ups. When I was a kid, I had this thing about not stepping on a crack in the sidewalk, and like some others I know, I always have to go back into the house before I lock the door, to check this and that, to make sure all is okay. Crazy thing. I'm out the door, in the car, and I have to make sure - just make sure. Even then, I'm asking my partner, did she or I do this or that, just to make sure. Here I am, sitting with you in the park, and I'm thinking, "Did I turn off the stove, the lights, and flush the toilet?"

"That is a dilemma. Maybe you should think about what one guy said,

"Life can only be understood backwards, but it must be lived forwards." 59

"I'm not sure what that means?"
"Neither am I. Most likely those geese over there, see them, I bet that has never entered their heads either."

"Say, back to that competition thing. The other day, I read somewhere about two guys, scientists, who were competing to see who could come up with a vaccine for polio. Both had what it takes to make it, but they were at loggerheads as to how it should be taken into the body. One said by needle, the other by spoon. It turned out that, after all the fighting, and waste of energy, squabbling about that in the newspapers, radio, and so on, both ideas were used, patients got both. Now doesn't that beat all. That sure seems different than how creatures other than ourselves get things done."

19

Ending It All

The plaque on the bench read, " In memory of Sandy Kurushimu." The man sat down and stared at the path, green grass, the hard boulders leaning on each other in a row, and then, lifting his tired blood shot tearful eyes, he watched. The waves frothed up spilling over the rocks as water from an overflowing sink. His tears, too, urged him to do something. It had to stop. He felt frightened. So much had gone wrong. So often it had gone wrong. He stood, heard a "Good morning." Felt a snuffling mop-faced dog nose his pant leg. No! He hoped the dog wouldn't lift his leg and pee. He felt abused enough.

The warmth of the sun on his head didn't rid him of the cold darkness within as he strode towards the weather-stained bridge. Looking over the rail he again watched, now not the unmanageable waves, but some ducks. They lightly bobbed about on the unpredictable waves, seemingly so effortless. He watched and he stared. A duck's head, then breast, would disappear, briefly mooning him with its rump before disappearing below the tormented surface. For a moment he felt anxious thinking, "Don't be silly, it will surface. Ducks always do."

But, no, minutes passed, One duck maybe gone, a body to mingle with the mud, forever. Then, popping up, it shook itself, and again effortlessly bobbed about, before submerging again.

An hour passed, and then two. The black cloud within him began to fade away. The urge ended, to jump, gag on water, to end it all, and be remembered as someone who couldn't swim among the sharks.

He heard steps on the bridge behind him, a dog's yelp, and a voice loud, nearby, and then fading, "Good day."

"Yes, he whispered, "It's now a good day." He turned, crossed over the bridge, and resolved to again to get his personal ducks in line while remembering the lesson learned watching ducks from the bridge in the park.

His wife must be frantic. He'd been away from home and office for hours. Get to a telephone, call his wife. Yes, that's what he would do first, and say, "I'm okay now, I'm okay!"

The two on the bench kept talking about what makes people do what they do, especially when they think about throwing in the towel.

One repeated that old saw, "When things, get tough, the tough get going."

The other, more of a deep thinker, had his opinions about what motivates people. That "m" word was one he liked. Out came a stream of concepts. He liked that "s" word, too.

"Survival, that's it. People will do anything to survive."

"Okay, "said his friend, "But what about the guys who want to end it all?"

"Oh, sure, there are a few exceptions."

"Territorialism, that's another reason people do what they do. That's what motivates them to get pushy with each other. Something that even birds and animals have in common with humans."

"That's true, "said his friend, "but humans have common sense enough to accept that 'live and let live' is the way to go."

"You may be partly right, but what about all the wars, most caused because some wanted bigger parts of the pie, and started wars to get more land."

"I can buy into that, I suppose, but I think the bottom line is simple. People do what they do because they live between two experiences, pain and pleasure, and the goal is to dissolve or avoid pain, and they'll do anything to avoid pain."

"Birds and animals, they're the same."

"One other thing though, that sets us humans apart is that birds and animals don't try, like we do, to keep from getting bored. Relieving boredom and avoiding pain, may really be, when you come right down to it, why people do what they do."

"Boredom is the feeling that everything is a waste of time; serenity, that nothing is." 60

"Boy, that's heavy!"

His friend, remembering some of his college learning nodded, and added, "Yes, but it's more complicated than that. Humans have four basic needs they have to satisfy: security, recognition, responses from people, hopefully good strokes, and at least some new adventures to have, and be able to tell others about them. How does that sound? Does that make sense?"

"Yes, but I've heard it said a little differently."
"How so?"
"Well, there is this guy called Victor Frankl, a psychologist who said that to have meaning in life is the ticket. A guy needs something that keeps him going, no matter what. If he doesn't have anything to live for, he won't."

"I suppose that's true." yawned his friend, "but you forgot that there are imaginary needs and real needs." He learned that from a TV distant learning program.

His friend, not enthralled with that thought, and not knowing where to go with that, decided to change the conversation to get at how people connect with each other, thinking that has a lot to do with why people do things.

His friend, not wanting to leave any stone unturned said, "Hold on, you forget that people with their heads screwed on right will seek to find their centre. From there they can work on getting their acts together." He had done some pottery, and knew that if you didn't centre the clay, it would go all wonky as you tried to pull up a cylinder, and the end result, if there was one, would be grotesque, and not what was meant to be.

His partner, sharing the bench with him, said, "It sound's like you're getting religious on me. The next thing you're going to say is that, we're spiritual creatures, unlike birds and animals."
"That may be!"

"Well, forget that, at least for now. Let's get back to the idea that people do what they do to get along with each other. That old book by Dale, somebody or other, "How to Win Friends and Influence People" maybe puts a finger on it. Because, you know, each of us is not one person, but three, the one we think we are, the one other people think we are, and the person we really are."

"So what has that to do with how much tea there is in China?"
"Well, look, a guy has to know how he is coming across as a person with others in order to get on track on what he's to do in rubbing shoulders with people."
"So, we need others to tell us who we are. The next thing you're going to say is, that we need others to tell us where to go."

"Look, forget that idea. After all, what it comes down to is this, it's really dog against dog. The fittest survives. That's what all those survival shows on TV are really about.

They are like mirrors to show us we're not much different than all of nature's other creatures. Just look at any sport. Take hockey for example. Using fancy terms, the game is like life, participation is all pervasive, a social phenomena, based on elimination by competition, and you can't get away from it. The idea is to be the last standing on top of the hill.
"Each person needs skill sets to survive. In hockey it's character, team work, and good work ethics. Same in life. So you can say all you want, but what motivates people, makes them tick is to compete, to survive, and if possible, with the right stuff, be top dog."

After his friend gave his spiel, his partner on the bench said,
"I've heard it said more nicely, be the best that you can be, and remember the ones who succeed are standing on the shoulder of others who made their success possible."
His friend, having the last word, said, "Enough! You're bringing tears to my eyes. Let's go have coffee, see what's new."

20

Self Care

    Goose Island Park gave those gathered there the chance to share great truths through their actions. Huffing and puffing, hunched over runners, heads up speeders who could talk while running, and comfortable joggers passed determined, straining, red-faced walkers, and casual visiting en-route travellers circumventing the park's lake. All in motion made a statement, whether conscious of it or not, one by the ancient Greek Herophilus,
    "When health is absent, wisdom cannot reveal itself, art cannot manifest, strength cannot fight, wealth becomes useless, and intelligence cannot be applied."
    Others, lounging on the grass, pronounced another sometimes neglected truth,
    "Rest is not idleness, and to lie sometimes on the grass under trees on a summer's day, listening to the murmur of the water, or watching the clouds float across the sky, is by

no means a waste of time." 61

Amplifying that observation is the need expressed in a simple but profound way,

"Just living is not enough. One must have sunshine, freedom, and a little flower." 62

Some persons who found both time and zeal, showed they believed it wasn't an either-or decision between leisure or physical exertion on the path. For they showed in doing both, that they believed:

"True enjoyment comes from activity of the mind and exercise of the body; the two are ever united." 63

It was true that, for some, it was all that they could do to make it around the park while gasping for breath, which verified the idea that,

"To be or not to be isn't the question. The question is how to prolong being." 64

There was, of course, another alternative to running out of steam while circling the lake. The seldom used scout pace that involves alternating running steps with walking steps might help the determined oxygen-starved.
Beside the presence of the oxygen starved, there are others that, though they can get around the lake without a call for an ambulance, suffer another impediment.

A spectator watched the people making their way around the lake. His interest in communication caused him to conclude that eye contact with others, meeting and passing varied, and that, unless the persons on the path went out of their way to do so, it was no different than when rushing pedestrians on downtown streets stared right through those whom they brushed by.

    One observation that he made did ring a positive note for him. Many languages were spoken by people visiting with each other as they went along. He thought such expressed and, in a way, celebrated the freedom Canadians have to belong, retain their uniqueness of culture and language, and to be happy.

21

The Lecturer's Lone Listener

A college professor thought he'd get away from the campus and have his lunch at the park, sit under a tree, and maybe rehearse his afternoon lecture to the birds. Why not? He found his favourite tree, sat with his back to it, and let his thoughts shuffle into some semblance of order around the topic of loneliness. Since it was a first year class, he'd keep his lecture simple.

Loneliness, a feeling we all experience sometimes. Let's think about it and ways to overcome it. It's been said that,
"We reach the crisis stage in feeling lonely when we open our junk mail and actually read it."

Loneliness is nothing new. Artists have expressed the loneliness of people. Rene Magritte, the artist, shows the head of man and woman about to kiss, but their heads are covered by cloth bags. George Tooker, another painter, shows people in a subway lurking about in isolation, staring with fear at each other. Edward Munch shows people in a deathbed scene with their backs turned to one another.

Great thinkers speak of loneliness. Dr. Paul Tournier, Swiss psychologist, claimed;
"Loneliness is the most devastating malady of the age."
He and others claim, "The ravages of loneliness reach deeply into many of our most vexing problems."

Loneliness strikes every age:

-children whose parents have little time for them; teens who feel misunderstood and alienated
-married couples who feel estranged from partners even when living together intimately.

-The aged who feel useless and unwanted, yet have so much to offer
- even, yes, politicians.

Persons can feel very alone even when surrounded by people. A poet and novelist wrote on "solitude:"

"Loneliness is most acutely felt with other people, for with others, we suffer from our differences, differences of taste, temperament, and mood."

Another novelist, Faith Baldwin claimed;

"Loneliness can pierce you like a knife on a spring morning or a golden summer afternoon, no matter where you are or what you are doing."

So who can deny that loneliness haunts all.

What Causes Loneliness?

The deepest cause of loneliness is our human condition itself. Someone said, "We were born to be alone."

Loneliness is not a new human experience. Remember Robinson Crusoe and his longing for a human companion? Author Defoe expressed all our longings for companionship, connection, and hope in the person of Robinson Crusoe.

Tennessee Williams in his play "Orpheus Descending" wrote, "We've got to face it, we're under a lifelong sentence to solitary confinement inside our own lonely skins for as long as we live on this earth."

Why does that have to be? Remember the Bible's Adam who represents humankind. His life illustrated the cause of loneliness for even when he was united with Eve.

Genesis(2:18)

They still found themselves out of harmony with the Creator and creation, and thus were still lonely.

What impact does loneliness have upon humans and how people try to deal with it?

There are just too many people that are lonely too often. Loneliness seeps from the pores of our culture.

Look. The personal columns in newspapers and magazines are often filled with intimate personal ads from persons seeking friends or partners. Now, the internet does the trick. Look also at Company ads which pick up on this social ailment of loneliness. One telephone company advertisement read, "Reach out and touch someone." The electronic church plays on the vulnerability of the lonely. Real estate firms sell condos advertising them as " real places where you make friends."

The lonely feeling is a button for ad-makers to push to make persons buy, claiming it is the answer to loneliness.

Think of ways humans use to drain away the feeling of loneliness.

Accumulate: Tennessee Williams wrote a play called "The Glass Menagerie" The play about escaping reality has Amanda Wingfield retreating into an illusory world of her youth. She loves her children, but her constant nagging and her constant retelling of her romantic stories are too much for her daughter, Laura. It also drives away her son, Tom. Laura Wingfield, the crippled daughter, takes refuge among her glass figurines, the glass menagerie. The figures become a symbol of her retreat from reality and loneliness.

Keep striving, another way. In Arthur Miller's "Death of a Salesman:"
Biff: "Are you content, Hap? You're a success aren't you? Are you content? Happy? "
Hap: "Why no, Biff."
Biff: "Why? You're making money, aren't you?"
Hap: "All I can do now is wait for the manager to die. And suppose I get his position. He's a good friend of mine. He just built a terrific estate on Long Island. He lived there about two months and he sold it. Now he's building another one. He can't enjoy it once it's finished. And I know that's just what I'd do. I don't know what I'm working for. Sometimes I just sit in my apartment, all alone. And I think of the rent I'm paying. And its crazy. But then, it's what I always wanted. My own apartment, a car, and plenty of friends. And still...I'm lonely."

Keep company with another lonely person to stem off haunting loneliness .
A Canadian poet and humorist, when a youth on lonesome nights, finding the hours intolerably long, would

dial long-distance directory assistance for some remote obscure place. Just as bored or lonely, the operator would chat with him about marriage or the weather, pleased at the human contact.

Keep Busy. When single a young man in an isolated place, not among his own ethnic group, kept busy thinking he could ward off loneliness as store manager, dispenser of medicine, weather reporter, school teacher, and local preacher. But he was still very lonely.

Feel sorry for others, thinking them lonelier than you. Tourists visiting a remote cove and taking pictures, asked a local,
"How can you live so far away from everything and be so content?"
The local answered , "Folks, you don't see me rushing to the city to take your picture as you're doing mine, do you?"

What do you think, do any or all of these do the "What then are the ways ?"

The professor looked around, up into the trees, shifted his body to stretch to look behind him, shrugged, and thought geese, some of those birds chattering away, no different than the kids in my big classes.

He didn't notice a lone figure lurking nearby who had seemed to be listening, even shaking his head and mouthing a "no" when the professor asked the birds and trees whether the loneliness eliminators that he'd mentioned were effective or not.

Getting up, stretching, throwing his lunch wrappers in a nearby bin, not noticing his one human audience, he returned to his tree, sat with his knees almost up to his chin, and began again to lecture.

So what then are the most effective ways to alleviate loneliness? Pausing for answers... none, just like in class? He pushed forward-

"First - Recognize loneliness for what it is, something that sours and sickens the spirit, something that can't be made a friend, or is seen as the pits. Preoccupation with loneliness is self- poisoning.

Second - Learn the difference between loneliness and aloneness. To be alone is neither good nor bad.
How we use our times of solitude will determine if it is good or bad.
    A widow cried, "Being alone does so colour one's life."
    Another widow replied, "But isn't it nice that we can choose our own colour."

Third - Remember, it is okay to be alone. Productive people seek solitude. It is often necessary to be alone in order to create. Everyone needs periods of aloneness.

Fourth - Try creative aloneness. Aloneness is necessary, not only to be creative or to get over the loss of a friend or loved one, but to regenerate.

    "An author found that he was running dry. He couldn't think or write. He had lost his gift. He couldn't function. He felt as though he was having a nervous breakdown. He went to his doctor for a prescription. The doctor told him to go to the ocean and open four envelopes, one every three hours.
    At 9 a.m. he opened the first. The note said, 'Listen.' For three hours he listened to the waves, the birds, the people. He listened to sounds that he hadn't heard in years.
    At 12 noon he opened the second envelope.'Try to Reach Back' the note said. For three hours he tapped his memory about where he had been and what he had done with his life.

At 3 p.m. he opened the third envelope. 'Remember your original motives. For three hours the author asked; Why did I start? Would I do it again? Why did I do that? Say that? React that way?'

At 6 p.m. the author opened the last envelope. It said, 'Write your worries in the sand.' For three hours he wrote his resentments, worries, and fear in the sand. Then he watched the waves roll in and wash them all away. That is solitude. That is renewal. That is creative aloneness." anon

We are called to be alone together, neither so private that we miss our responsibilities, nor so work-orientated that we miss solitude.

Fifth - Learn more about persons such as those who write history by their actions. By doing so you will find it is possible to take a strong stand on something, often running against the stream and, yet, surviving.

"Thank God for the lonely of this earth... the stark and oft-times naked and tragic figures who dared to stand alone - with God (whether they knew of his presence or not), and, standing alone with God, proved themselves pioneers of a new and better day and thus put humankind forever under obligation to them. When they were most alone, they were strongest." W.F.Kosman

Sixth - Involve self in service.
"Seldom can a heart be lonely if it seeks a lonelier still, self forgetting, seeking only empty cups to fill." anon

All about us are empty cups. Try filling them and watch your loneliness evaporate, said Billy Graham.

Seventh- Finding a family-like community. Sometimes we can have more in common than with a blood family far away. A psychologist claimed: "Community is the best answer to the universal sense of loneliness. In this life...the least lonely people I've met have joined some community... to feel they belong to something greater than themselves."

So, rising from the grass, brushing himself off, and hoping his lecture wasn't just for the birds, the professor moved off across the grass towards his car.

Still he didn't notice the silent, lone figure leave his outdoor lecture hall, and walk by himself, down a path, his head down, and hands shoved deep into his pockets. No one else seemed to notice him either.

22

Talk About Happiness

They were two middle aged women, now experiencing empty nests. Their children had, as one said, "Flown the coop."
One, sighing wistfully, said, "The kids made me happy, at least most of the time. Now what?"

The other, a real gung-ho outdoor type said,

"Happiness, you know, has a whole lot to do with getting in touch with oneself in relationship to nature. Take this park for example. I once read that happiness is one long continuous chain of little joys, little whispers from nature, little rays of sunshine in our daily work."

"That sounds a bit soppy! "
"Yes, I guess, maybe, but heck. Anyway, you can have a lot of fun, whether it's here in the park or at home, even

when you don't know you're having it. I read about a three year old. She was helping her mom bake a cake. Mom stirred while the girl added water and eggs to the mixture. As she was about to add the vanilla, she glanced up at mom with a grin and whispered gleefully,"Are we making a mess?"

Her friend, swallowing the story, said, "Oh stop, now you're reminding me of my kids again, and the home stuff with them."

"Okay, then look at it this way. You see that person ahead of us, being pushed in a wheel chair."

"So?"

"Well, when I taught school, I shared stories with the kids about the idea that you don't need to rely on circumstances to make you happy. I remember that story about Lord Byron and Sir Walter Scott . Both were lame. Byron was downright miserable with his lameness. He brooded on it till he loathed it. He never entered a public place, and sure not a park. For him, he didn't see any way that he could get any more buzz out of life. Much of the zest of living was gone.

"Scott, on the other hand never complained. He never spoke a bitter word about his disability, not even to his closest friend. It's not surprising that one day Scott got a letter from Byron that concluded,

"Scott, I would give my fame, to have your happiness."

"Well, thanks for that. It's a good story, but what about us? We're not the kind that anyone will remember, like those big guns."

"Okay, maybe we're not the heavyweights of society."

"Stop right there, and that's another thing, trying to be happy and lose weight at the same time doesn't make one happy."

"I'm not talking about that. I'm remembering someone else. I don't know whether she had a weight problem or not, or whether, if she were still alive, could or couldn't make it around the park without gasping for air. But what I do remember is that she, Louisa May Alcott, wrote at age 12 in her diary:

"Had good dreams and woke now and then to think, and watch the moon, I had a pleasant time with my mind, for it was happy."

"See, there you are, it doesn't take much to make a person happy. We can be happy right here, in this park. Sure there's no moon out, though I saw a faint glimpse of one early this morning, but you and I have lots of good stuff around us, the grass, birds, trees, a whole lot of stuff to think about, and enjoy. So let's get with it."

Her friend, not totally convinced, turned and said, "Just like that, eh, so simple. I'm not convinced. Even though I'm in the park where everything seems so fresh and vibrant, and the reflections in the water that today looks like glass, don't mirror me. Why is it that it takes so much convincing to get women to realize that they don't have to feel they need to remain eternally young to be happy? Look at that guy over there, the one with the paunch and the sweats. It's just like a man to see that he doesn't need to pretend that he's not over the hill."

"Yes, that's true. Somewhere in one of my movie magazines, I read about one actor who said,

"I may not have lived wisely, industriously, virtuously, but I have lived happily. I am not an introspective man, but I am, I hope, a grateful one. Life has treated me kindly, and should she suddenly withdraw her favours, I hope I shall always be mindful that for over 50 years the sun shone on my back."
"Sounds a bit corny."

"Maybe, but it can't be any more maudlin than this bit that I read in some self improvement book - I can't remember which one - I think I've just about read them all.

"Who then are the happy ones?"

'The happy are those who know how to live with the unknown without feeling threatened or frightened. The happy are those who accept the unknown, even seek the unknown - Willing to face the unknown allows one to meet a wide variety of people easily and naturally regardless of age, education, class or colour.

The happy are those who know that there is no adventure without uncertainty.

The happy are also the grateful.

The happy are those who appreciate. The happy appreciate again and again the basic goods of life, however stale these experiences may be to others.'

"You know that culvert that they were digging up the other day? Well, when I jogged by the guys digging around there, I thought of one of my profs... I think he's dead now, who said,

"There was this economist. He was watching a workman digging a ditch. He look at how the dirt kept the shape of the shovel as it flew through the air and landed exactly where the workman wanted it. Like an apprentice approaching a master, the economist joined the workman and practised shovelling until he had learned the knack. "

"Okay I got the drift of that, but are there any more of your goodies, the happy are stuff?"

"Yes, a couple more. Do you like them?"

"What's to like? I just thought that you were happy spieling them off; I didn't want to spoil your fun."

" Well, if that's the little you're getting from them, I'll stop right there."

"No, please go on, you've got my attention. I'm with you."

"The happy are people with a mission in life who aren't self centred. Happiness for them is the by-product of work and duty. Maybe this is the reason why mothers with babies don't get sick as often as other people.

The happy are also the Realists who are able to detect the fake, the dishonest. They don't look through life with rose-coloured glasses or through glass darkly. They see what is there rather than their own wishes, hopes, fears. They don't complain about water because it's wet, or rocks because they're hard, or a competitor because he beats them to a contract. Why? Because they see people as they really are and thus are seldom disappointed in others.

The happy don't blink at ills and injustices around them; but neither do they believe that the world can be set right overnight through social and political panaceas.

Happy persons like to do useful productive work, to use their abilities fully to enjoy helping people, but they are not door mats. They tend to be self-sufficient and can enjoy both solitude and company but aren't dependent on either.

Though tolerant of people's minor flaws, happy persons dislike cruelty and destructiveness. Healthy persons have no hang-ups about prosperity and refuse to participate in other people's negative emotions or cling to their own."

"Where did you say you got that list from?"
"I can't remember. I read a lot of stuff. I also remember reading about a pilot."
"And what was that about?"
"It seems there was this pilot trapped in the desert for two days. He found an orange in his plane wreck. Stretched out beside the fire he looked at the orange and said to himself that men did not know what an orange is. Here he was condemned to die, he thought to himself. Still the certainty of dying couldn't compare with the pleasure he was feeling. The joy he took from that orange in his hand was one of the greatest joys he'd ever known." anon

"Isn't that something?"

"So what you're saying, and what it all comes down to is this, "Thank God for small mercies."

"Bertrand Russell claimed that to be without some of the things you want is an indispensable part of happiness.
See, I read, too."
" Hurrah for you. I think you got it. I don't know what movie star it was, but she said, I think it was her:

'We're made for enjoyment and the world is filled with things which we can enjoy, unless we are too proud to be pleased with them or too grasping to care for what we receive.'

"I guess that's something like I found in a book called "The River" by R.Goodens. One person in the book asked the other, 'How can I be happy?' Her friend answered, 'It isn't for us to dictate (or something to that effect). If you are happy, you are. You can't make yourself unhappy.

We 're something, part of something, larger than ourselves. That's what I read. I guess it's something like being part of this park, do you think? "

"I guess it is. Just try to tell my perfectionist, self- made man, ex-husband about it. My pastor a few Sunday's back - I got a copy of his sermon, quoted from a guy called Gerald Kennedy.
"A young married man had read all the psychoanalytic and religious self-help books on how to adjust to life, marriage and to other difficulties. His young wife, who had tried to live up to the precepts in all these books one day rebelled: 'Now that we've found real happiness, couldn't we have some fun too?' "

"It sounds like, somehow you got the wrong deal, if you thought that you were deprived of fun like that young woman in your story."

"Not really. He's still got his hang-ups. I'm getting in the zone, like a hockey goalie - you like hockey? Never mind. Now, since we split, I'm like the lady in Thornton Wilder's play "Our Town." This person did get a second chance.
She had died, but was given the opportunity to live one day of her life. I've got more of course. Experiencing human existence for the second time, she saw how marvellous it was. When the time came to leave forever, she said farewell to previous small miracles that she barely noticed when she was alive. I guess, like those I'm noticing in the park and in other places where there is so much free stuff, to see and take in."

"Happiness,"as one poet said is," made up of minute fractions - the little, soon-forgotten, the sight of two children sitting on a log talking and eating apples. The smell of pine gum warming in the bright afternoon sun." anon
"Just look around you, right? "
"Right!"

23

The Boy and His Teacher

She stood, one hand finger-spread on the sweaty, sticky cover of the new biology text. She stared at the windowless walls, and remembered the spruce scented air, and the lake's freedom-loving breeze. School halls and classrooms had a heavy soiled smell, tainted by pungent loose-laced runners; so expensive, the latest style, yet so boring. From hair tossed back in the breeze, arms swung wide, elated dance through summer, she now gazed at the wall clock. It shared the light of the cold fluorescents shining on baseball cap-headed boys, and mid-riff, bare-bellied girls. Thinking that they too, needed a gradual sinking into the seats for another heavy semester, she heard her self say,
   "Class, as planned, we are going over to the park to gather water specimens to use this semester. " She glanced around the class, trying to break up the cliquey scrums, and rouse the sleepy singles with her voice and eyes. For a moment the thought took the shape of a picture, the park's lake giving urine-like specimens to the clinically trained.

   The idea of breaking out of the dry-walled classroom got the desks scraping, feet shuffling, and a scramble for the door. Then, "Hold on, pick up the jars and dip nets.

I'll meet you at the dock."

As she walked toward the park, she thought of the reflective time that she had had that summer at the cottage by another lake, one where haunting loon calls echoed off surrounding hills. There, she often sat on the end of the dock, paddling her bare feet in the cool, clear water, and brushing away pesky mosquitoes and flies.

Every year, with her escape from the classroom, came encounters, not only with pesky insects, but with persistent thoughts that urged attention.

Biology, dissecting of the bodies of frogs, that resembled human physiology, though visceral, was a snap compared to dissecting one's thoughts to reveal haunting conundrums common to her and her friends.

Without fail, pesky problems kept her summers from being pure earthy joy. They drove her to seriously reflect on life. She was often alone. Her week-end visitors returning to their city jobs left her talking out loud, making one-way conversation with nature's living things, the begging squirrel and the sheltering tree. Her thoughts transformed into words mingled with the other sounds drifting down from the canopy of green above her shake-roofed cottage, its front yard a sandy beach.

Like Goose Island Park that had the power to lift off the shelves of one's mind dusty or mouldy memories or unresolved issues - so also did her creature comfort sanctuary do the same.

Like stuff hidden and neglected in frig, drawer, or cupboard, much, every summer, seemed to whisper, do you want to keep us, or pitch us from your mind.
And, like every summer, she would try again to clear her

head, and begin with an uncluttered mind to grope around in the minds of the latest version of the young hormone-driven, concerned about zits and, "am I all right" feelings.

Oh, she thought, if only we human creatures could give up indulging in self-consciousness and self doubt. True, there's other things we keep on the shelves in our minds that we could easily do without. No! Should do without. When I get back at it in September, there will be a new horde of kids invading my lab and my seat of emotions. And a bunch will be tormented within by feeling of envy, their brains not yet able to settle their self images as being okay.

Throughout her thought journey, nature's orchestra musicians, birds, frogs, and insects supported her in the ongoing sorting process. In her apartment, she'd shove a CD into her player, but no sounds match those of nature. Even the faint thundering and sheet lightning, beginning to give legitimacy to the dark bloated clouds moving into her visual space, helped by compressing her thoughts into an oozing, fruitful mass of ideas to work through.

How, when she got back to school, could she convince the teens to risk a little more, to give up the security blankets of peer acceptance, and begin to grow out of their awkwardness. And perhaps, where and if it surfaces, cruel crowd mass hysteria?

Would it help by supplying them with images such as the Peanuts cartoon's Linus dragging around his security blanket, woven from the inferior threads of poor self-esteem? Would they get the message?

Would she help by urging them to think about how we, as nature's other creatures, often are so self conscious and worried to death with an inferiority complex, that we can't even focus on what we are meant to do to reach our full potential as human beings?

When she got back would she try again to get across the idea that it's no good to envy others? Would it help if she told them one story that she had read - about the singer Buffy St. Marie who used voice, personality, money, and fame to help her native people, and how she tells of her first ambition to be a blond cheerleader, then an airline stewardess like the average girl. But as an average girl she failed. So she decided to be herself!

Her thoughts about what she would do differently to try to encourage her students to keep their minds on their work, to be less distracted by self consciousness, doubt, and fear of rejection, kept her in the indoors of her mind, rather than outward to enjoy the rain-freshened air.

How, she asked herself, could she inject a breath of fresh air into the minds of those kids who feel rejected by their peers, who dump their doubts and fear on them through snide remarks and cruel ganging-up. How would she be able to get across to the lonesome abused that it is not their doing as the put-down, but the abuser's hang-ups that are stirring the pot.

How, she thought, could she get across to the down-and-outer kids that often what is said to them by kinder people as constructive criticism, doesn't have to be thought of as one's whole person being under attack, that a person's worth is not dependent on others' remarks, suggestions, or language.

She remembered reading in the Digest something that she found helpful. Maybe she'd share that with her students too. There is no reason for anyone to feel inferior. Some, without even knowing it, demonstrate not inferiority, but a sense of false pride. A patient who shared his state of mind stated without hesitation, "I just can't help it doctor if my inferiority complex is bigger and better than anyone else's !"

She thought, that is pretty neat stuff, but remembered something even neater. One of her high school teachers once told her that no one can take the role of playwright and stage manager in our lives. We should not depend on others to give us worth.

As she sat bailing the water out of her boat at the cottage after a cloud burst, she thought it incredible that certain bits of stuff that she had read beyond the professional material, often surfaced to fill her consciousness with useful stuff to share with her students. She seldom remembered where she read it, or who said it, but it still seemed right to share.

That time at the cottage, when she was doing her away from the city stock-taking of where she was going with life and her teaching, she also remembered a story of a teacher who asked each of her students to take a sheet of paper and list all his or her good points as a young person. One child put up his hand and said, "Teacher, can I use both sides of the paper?"

In her years of teaching she came to the conclusion, as many teachers have, that unless some students can clear their minds from feeling like real clumsy klutzes, they will never have sufficient healthy empty space in their thoughts to learn.

Her flashbacks to her summer at the cottage came to an abrupt end. Her feet found their way down the path to the pier. She hadn't realized how she had dawdled. All her students were already there, their bodies lounging on the grass, some leaning over the water, nudging and pushing, while their young eyes, teeth, and mouths shaped an array of feelings, boredom, brazenness, eagerness, and confusion.

Now their leader had arrived they began their cool, nonchalant drifting over to where she stood with her clipboard. She rattled off her instructions, polished by long use, and tried, using her bag of verbal tricks, to rouse the troops to action. The goal to fill the jars with scummy water, "Visually inspect the contents for signs of life, record your findings, share with others, and after a half an hour, meet me back at the lab."

Off they went, looking like bear cubs swatting the water for fish, maybe awkwardly, like young deer cautiously and vigilant, dipping graceful necks to lap water. She abruptly stopped her brief fantasizing, and mumbled to herself - "not likely."

Now, she watched and listened to the chatter, shouts and laughter. All seemed to be moving about in clumps, all except one lean awkward youngster, who held back, balancing on the rocks, seeming to absentmindedly poke away at the water with a wooden-handled dip net. The others paid no attention to him. She began walking toward him. He either didn't seem aware of her approaching, or just didn't care.

"What did you find Louis?"

"Loo," he mumbled.

"Oh yes, Loo. Anything interesting?"

"I don't know what to do," he spat the words between his almost closed lips, while briefly glancing over at her.

His grey peaked face, tired eyes, faded straw coloured hair down around his ears and teasing the collar of a thrift-store jacket, softened what she, his teacher, was about to say next.

She remembered some of what she had recalled during her summer at the cottage. She went over to a bench, patted the seat, saying "Forget the dip net, let's talk." She didn't try to pry him open to get at what was bugging him. His distance from the group made that perfectly clear.

She didn't feel bad when his awkwardness muzzled his mouth from sharing his obvious pent-up feelings of worthlessness, smoldering hurt. She knew a little about this boy from school records, and from the other teachers.

So she talked softly, and he appeared to listen willingly. "Loo, I knew of a teacher once who asked one of her young pupils, 'What was the most valuable invention in the world? You know what he answered, Loo?"

"No. Don't. "

"The little guy answered, 'Me!' "

"How can he say that?" Loo leaned over towards her, then quickly, as before, peered down at his worn and torn runners.

"Loo," she touched him briefly - not supposed to do that now - "You can say that too, because you, me, we're all that way. Really!"

He rubbed one foot over the other, still staring down, and whispered, "I don't think so."

"Well, it's true, Loo. Believe it. You know Loo, I heard somewhere, and I believe it to be true, that what gives a great person worth is not what others think of him, but the cause that he identifies with. If the cause is trivial, merely self serving, then, it will not be surprising if the person thinks poorly about himself. There's an old expression, maybe your grandmother used it, Hitch your wagon to a star. That still holds true."

"I don't got a grandmother. I got an uncle who played hockey once. Good at it too."

"What did you hear him say about all this?"

"He didn't."

"How come, Loo?"

"He's dead; shot himself."

Before he broke that news, she had planned to go on with, "It's so sad that some persons, driven by their own feelings of inadequacy, will go to great lengths to achieve. They often fail, not because they do not have worth, but because they have chosen the wrong vocation, calling, or venture; a square peg in a round hole."

It is also sad that society rewards people, such as

athletes, with big bucks, expecting them to become miracle workers, driving them to the point of exhaustion, believing that they can buy them and trade them like cattle. But, it is wonderful that people will give others the opportunity to fail, and learn from their mistakes, even trust them with very important responsibilities.

My God, she thought what am I thinking anyway! Loo straightened up, turned, touched her shoulder lightly, looked up into her eyes glistening with a film of tears, and he lip-shaped silent words.

He knew.

24

Hugs Are Miracles Too

The two, a crusty grey-mustached man, obviously the father of the other, a slim, fast walker, looked about, commenting back and forth as they rounded the lake.

The older one pointed to a pathetic looking gander, looking tired and arthritic, barely making it over the rocks and onto the grass.

"You see that, don't think he'll be joining the ones heading south this fall. Don't think I'll make it either. It'll be a miracle if I even make it through the winter here. Damn prostrate!"

"You never know," the younger said. "Miracles do happen."

The old man coughed, "Seems the only time a miracle happens is when someone wins the 649 lottery."

"Oh, I don't know about that, I think it just depends on how you define a miracle."

"Getting academic on me, next thing you know you're going to use big words again."

"Maybe, big thoughts, but big words...no, I don't think so. I can believe that a miracle takes place when something very extraordinary has taken place, seldom happens, and when it does, it is to only a very special few, the odds being a million to one."

"Well," coughing again, "that cuts me out. I ain't no special person."

"To me, you are. And sometimes miracles happen, and we may just not have taken notice. They happen all around us throughout our lives and cannot be considered trivial. Birth, that's a miracle. Our very lives, fragile as they are, are miracles. Recovery from an illness is a miracle, the changing of a life is a miracle."

"Yeah, okay, but just suppose I don't make it, beat this crappy cancer, does that mean, no miracle for me?"

"Look, sometimes, you know, the miracle for us is something that we didn't even think about happening, something altogether different from what we wanted, but still super good."

"Well, that's fine son. I guess I can live with that...at least as long as I'm around. I have heard a lot around the table down at Timmy's about` miracles,' as some of the guys put it, ones that we can all be thankful for, health or no health."

His son, feeling his dad warming up to the idea that miracles, of a sort, do happen, dumped the whole bale of ideas that he had about miracles.

"Dad, modern equipment with its sophisticated innards and fine tuned engineering is still vulnerable to break-down. It is a miracle that our bodies, so much more complex than the most sophisticated equipment, do as well as they do."

The father lifted himself painfully from the park bench, shuffled over to the rocks lining the lake. He stared bleary-eyed at some geese with their goslings, and with his back to his son, rasped, "I suppose them, too, miracles like us. You think, son?"

"Sure Dad, like us. Come on and sit back down. Now, as I was saying..."

"Would you say that fly buzzing around my head, bugging me, that's a miracle too?"

" Yes Dad, that too - now just as I was about to tell you, listen Dad. The point to consider is this. We as a people have advanced. But have we advanced so far that we can legitimately dismiss the evidence of miracles? Isn't it true that we know less, and understand less, about more and more?"

"Son, can you reach down and pick up that feather there. I wonder what bird that came off of? Would you know? Kind of like the Creator's writing instrument, do you think?"

"A bit far-fetched, Dad. Now getting back to what I was explaining to you. Science has performed miracles in keeping people alive longer. Penicillin has save many. Antibiotics have rescued even more from dreadful diseases. People who wear glasses survive. Would many of us have survived back then if physically handicapped or short sighted as we are now? Not likely. But has science improved the quality of life for those who live longer?" anon

The father said, "Do you want me to answer that?"

"No that's okay Dad. Let's get on with what I was saying. But of course scientists have not lost faith in the idea that miracles can and will occur. They still believe that the impossible is going to happen and the incredible predicted will turn out to be true. For instance, the sun, astronomers say, is cooling off, burning itself out, and millions or billions of years from today it will die, leaving this earth with no heat.

People, they say, will either crawl deep into the bowels of the earth closer to the raging heat of the centre of the earth's core or they will move off to other habitable planets, if such exist."

The dad, oblivious to his son's words, peered out at the weed-woven surface of the water, and said, "You know son, my body will soon be part of the mud for water plants to grow in this lake. You are going to scatter my ashes here as I asked you to do when I go. You did say you would, right?"

His son gave his dad a painful glance, and continued, "You know, Dad, our very existence on this planet is a miracle of the greatest proportions. What do you think about that, Dad? What do you say to that?"

His dad turned, peered into his face intently through bleary, tired eyes, and it was at that moment his son realized that his dad, who had been his teacher, and now had given over that role to him - his dad DID NOT HAVE HIS HEARING AIDS ON!

"Dad," the son shouted, "You tired? Want to walk some more, maybe talk some more before we head back to the lodge? Why don't we sit down right here?"

"Sure, okay, what were we talking about again?"

"Miracles, Dad, different kinds. You know across the centuries many deserts have been changed into productive places. Miracles!
I heard somewhere about a person, one of many, who after an ear operation, cried out, "Doctor, I can hear." The doctor had replaced the smallest bone in the human body, the stapes, with a wisp of stainless steel wire in a hearing apparatus implanted in the human ear, miniaturization. Wow!

But still, an even greater miracle yet, most have heard about this, one Dad. You have, Dad?"

No comment. His dad must be listening intently. He'd put his hearing aids on.

"Dad, so what do you think of that, Dad; Dad! Oh Dad, you'd fallen asleep. I'm sorry, what can I do for you?"

"Huh? Oh, you can give me a hug, son. I like hugs!"

25

It's Worth It

"In the depth of winter I finally learned that there was in me an invincible summer." 65

That unique kind of connectedness was not unique to people. Humans, gifted with the ability to think abstractly, and to find the use of symbolism to make sense of it all, could also accept without reservation that,

"Everything in Nature contains all the powers of Nature. Everything is made of hidden stuff." 66

That hidden stuff in humans surfaces as similar hopes and fears that cause people with that commonality to connect with each other, especially when they realize that they are part and parcel of all that is, and that,

"Nature is a collective idea, and, though its essence exists in each individual of the species, can never in its perfection inhabit a single object." [67]

If one makes an effort in the park to become aware of all that is gained through the senses, that person, receptive to the story the park tells, will realize the power humans have as complex beings to "make the deserts bloom and lakes die."

On the other hand, without that insight, one will miss the point.

"Lack of awareness of the basic unity of organism and environment is a serious and dangerous hallucination." [68]

One other perceptive person said with conviction, in speaking of this garden, our planet - of which this park is a minute part,

"We have nowhere else to go... this is all we have." [69]

It is somewhat unfortunate that the ecosystem, even that of a park, is vulnerable to human intervention. Some have said that spells disaster, based on the human species past reputation. For,

"The sun, the moon and the stars would have disappeared long ago, had they happened to be within reach of predatory human hands. " [70]

Still there is hope, for we humans have a choice. We do have, unlike the park's other creatures, a little power to plan, forecast the future, and take responsibility for our actions. It's also humbling to know that, somehow, regardless of what we do, we, like the rest of the park's creatures are not all powerful.

For, "a flower falls, even though we love it; and a weed grows, even though we do not love it." 71

Why, we sometimes wonder, why is that so? Could it be that, getting glimpses of a creative force at work, one can echo the thoughts inherent in these words?

"I've always regarded nature as the clothing of God." 72

A Creator, that in some mysterious way speaks to us in places like this park, connecting with us as one writer implied in this valid presumptuous way,

"I am a part of all you see in Nature: part of all you feel. I am the impact of the bee upon the blossom; in the tree I am the sap--that shall reveal the leaf, the bloom...that flows and flutes Up from the darkness through its roots." 73

26

One Bike, Two Bikes, More

Shuffling along the path circling the lake, he stopped by the park bench near the pavilion down wind from the dock. He lifted one leg, bent his knee, pressed his runner on the lip of the bench, and leaning over, pulled his right shoe laces to tie a tighter knot. Annoyed with having to often stop to tie the laces of that shoe, he indulged himself, as he often did, by analyzing the why of it.

Without fail, he blamed it on how his right foot was smaller his left, and his right leg bowed a bit, causing that foot, going along with the leg to pull unevenly on the lace. He had laboured in his head over the cause of his annoyance, one of many that he encountered on his trips around the park's lake. In each instance he dug around in his memory for answers to the causes of his inconveniences.

Not only did he do that, but, he contended with the

unexpected...Gee, see that, almost hit me a side blow with that bike, sometimes it's better to keep walking, running, or what have you. A moving target's harder to hit.

Laces tied, head up-like a hockey player- does one no good having your head down carrying a puck on your stick, you're bound to be hit hard - the same, with being deep in thought trying to untie knotty problems.

It seemed, unless a person got off the path, he was fair game for single-minded bike riders, and others moving fast, aided by mechanical human made devices. When fast bike pedallers, in-line skaters, or skate-boarders charge up from behind without warning, the startled walker had a split second to decide whether the threat would pass on the left or the right.

A guy get's the message that a person needs to be on one's toes when sharing the path, even in a supposedly pastoral park setting. You just never know when something is going to come at you. Stay alert, or you'll get hurt, the motto of fast pace livers who, restlessly driven, invade the sanctity of nature.

The one with the persistent dragging shoe laces did discover some people who, like the shoe which didn't match the other, stayed different. If anything they were more at home with nature, and more park- user friendly.

Off the beaten path, among the trees, some gathered around a table drinking tea. The smell of bannock and meat cooking on a nearby charcoal barbeque pleasantly scented the air, to tame the stench of rotting weeds sliming the surface of the lake's bay near the dock.

Laughing, tree climbing kids, wrestling rough- housing teens, infants, toddlers, mothers, and dads, if snap-shot photo-ed would catch a moment in time where a few native families, used to rural reserve life, would enjoy a respite from the concrete sterility and indifference of city streets.

As the shadows of approaching evening settled on the trees that created nature's temple canopied with a green leafed dome supported by branches, voices of the families' elders replaced the chorus of joking and kibitzing with tales of gritty living, spiked often with unexpected endings.

When one remember-when story began, it soon caught and held the attention of the drooping eyelid , blurred visioned, and the raven-haired bright eyed youth, who, intrigued, listened intently.

Remember when the coal-miners laboured underground, and lived good and bad times in this city. It was about then that a handful of friends had just crossed back over the border. They hadn't found work on the reserve. So they worked in the States, did a lot of overtime, and crossed back into Canada with a fat roll of money, twenty-thousand dollars to be exact. They were so darn happy, that they'd treated themselves to a stay in a motel instead of sleeping in their old rickety, fume-filled van. The only thing that was good about it was the new decoration on its top, a brand-new bike for a kid brother back on the reserve- a promise made, soon to be fulfilled.

Two days later, that dream, and some others, came crashing down. The friends were hauled out of their beds by ski-masked motel home-invaders. The intruders knew what they were after. They roughed up one friend who was forced to give them all the money he was carrying for the others. All but the very little spent, disappeared out the door, and was gone within minutes, followed by the roar of a hot truck engine.
The story teller, no doubt, must have been one of the unfortunate friends. For he dramatized his tale with first hand-like conversation. He said,
" You know it was just like it was yesterday. I can remember just about every word of our conversations about

that whole business."

"That was hell," one shouted.

"You telling me !"

"Worst than that, all that work for nothing," cried one.

"Heck, just when we think we're doing the right thing, telling welfare what they can do with their... we're back to square one," a third piped in.

The last friend who had been very quiet finally, bellowed, "It's worst than that. Remember we got that wacking big motel bill, no credit cards, and that beat up gas-guzzler out there. No telling whether, even if we wanted to make a quick get away, leaving bills behind us, we could have pulled that off. Besides, who wants that hassle, anyway."

The friends, down in the mouth, sprawled around the motel room, looking like death warmed up. Their silence, and the gloom that had settled on the room, was suddenly broken by the only one who had been pacing back and forth, swearing under her breath. She stopped. A faint smile formed on her tired face. The defeated look washed away, leaving a brighter, eye sparkling appearance.

Each of her friends sat up. One asked, "What gives. What are you looking so silly about. This is no laughing matter."

"Maybe, not, but then again," she answered. "I remember something. There was this guy in the restaurant, and the table across from us. He looked pretty interested in our roll of money that I peeled off some to pay the bill. I heard his name. His friend used it when they talked together. I got the idea, he and his buddy worked at the mine. Name was Keelo, I remember that because it was so different."
"So, how's that going to help? " asked her friend, elbow-propped up beside her.

"So we tell the police, that it's this Keelo who ripped us off. Then what? Even if he's still got the money, and the police get it from him, or from his buddy, how is that going to help us? How can we prove the money is ours?" one of the other motel - sharing friends asked.

"Well I just thought of something that I did when I first got charge of the money from you guys. I didn't tell you that I did it. You might have poked fun at me."

"So, what did you do," a couple of them laughed.

"You might not believe it, but well...I finger printed each bill with my mascara."

"You think that will do the trick, and get our money back." one chuckled. That would be one up on that white guy Keelo, if he's the rip-off artist."

"Worth a try. Let's get the police on board. Phone our own RCMP on the reserve. Don't know the ones here. And in the meantime, while he's getting his act together, let's check the local thrift store. Need a bike for my little guy back home. Got a few bucks left. Maybe get one cheap to replace the new one they stole off the top of the van," said the older of the friends, who looked a little more with it, less pessimistic.

The story teller was now getting into the good part. He looked around at his listeners, eager for more.

"I should have been on stage, eh? Quite a performance from an old geezer like me. Anyway, what happened next was this.

The RCMP got their man. He did it, and because the smart lady among those men had I.D.'d the money, they got most of it back. By the way, they got one rusty bike from the thrift store before hearing the good news. They fixed it up using the tools from the van, and some bits of paint and stuff. Sold it, bought a better one, and you can believe it or not, bought a couple more, piled them on the roof of the van, thick exhaust fumed it back to the reserve -and there's more! A couple of those characters, once down in the mouth, who had been ripped off- thought buying, fixing up and selling bikes was so much fun. Well, if you drive down the main drag on our reserve, you'll see a sign they're really proud of,

    "COMMUNITY BIKE STORE
     Get Your Bikes Here. Cheap."
    "That's some story!"
    "But that's not the end of it."

There is this guy - looks like Santa Claus. Call him the bike man. Live's off the reserve in another town. He collected antique bikes - even had one manufactured by John Deere. The bike store owners on the reserve bought his collection. If they hadn't it was just going to rust away. It seemed the town wasn't interested in helping him preserve and display them. But efforts didn't fall by the wayside.

    The bike store and museum on the reserve became something to behold, visited by many who found evidence of "We can do" has become, "We have done it!"

27

Though We See Through a Glass Dimly

Two high school friends, Mark and Beth, cut through the park on their way to and from school most weekdays. Their talk en route centred on the usual interests and troubles common to them and their peers. Shakespeare's Hamlet also kept cropping up in their conversations, seemingly uninvited - partly because it was required reading that semester, and even more so, because of that "To be or not to be" quote. It haunted their thoughts where the big questions of life roamed around begging for answers.

The two became very familiar with the park's natural furniture, so much so that only new additions would have had a chance of getting their attention, so preoccupied were they with their own teen interests.
During their high school years, using the park for a short-cut, they had noticed, and quickly shrugged off - dismissing from their minds, weird characters who appeared, and in time, disappeared. But one Friday afternoon on their

way home, they both heard something strange - a sound that just didn't blend in, nor contribute to the chatter they had become so accustomed to in the park.

It came from a fragile-looking, grey haired woman who, it appeared, was reading out loud to her dog. The teens casually moved closer, hoping the woman wouldn't be distracted and stop reading. She wasn't. They listened and heard,

"Hannah," Paul's voice sounded remote and spent but the tone predicted an important announcement.
"Hannah- I have been doing a great deal of thinking tonight...emergency thinking.. I've never taken much interest in the idea that the things we do and the things we believe can influence, in any way, whatever powers there may be - outside and beyond ourselves... and I'm not sure, even now, that I have any faith to offer. My mind is upset, and I know I'm not using it according to its habits. But so many people have believed - and do believe. I've been groping about to see if I could do it too. I have even tried to pray - but it has seemed an awful hypocritical thing for me to do.

                  Lloyd C Douglas in " White Banners."

The two soon nodded to each other that they had heard enough, and continued on their way, barely mentioning again what they had heard.

On Monday afternoon, to their surprise, the same woman sat reading to her dog, who looked up at her so attentively. In the weeks that followed, the woman, whom they had written off in their minds as just another eccentric, sat on the same bench reading out loud.

Many weeks passed with no change. Finally the teens just had to satisfy their curiosity. They had to find out something - anything, about the strange person who had become more than a mere park novelty.

So one late afternoon they sidled over to her bench, sat

down, and staring out at the lake, small talked their way into feeling more comfortable with her. To their surprise, she wasn't mad. In fact she seemed quite normal for an old person. After they had left the woman and her dog Plato and started home, they noted that if anything, their new acquaintance had a charismatic personality.

"Certainly not one like the witch that enticed juicy children into her gingerbread house," Beth said.

"What ever were you thinking? Mark laughed.

"I don't know, just kids stuff."

"You and I know we aren't kids. In fact we should be able to talk to this person. She seems to make sense. For fun, let's ask her about Hamlet's, "To be or not to be," Mark said, "that's one of life's big questions, right?"

So the next week, they got into a conversation with the interesting woman. It soon, again to their surprise, led to the unpacking of the "To be or not to be" question, and the whole business about beliefs, especially about a belief in a God.

The two found that their acquaintance became a friend whom they found credible. Her name was Priscilla. She was a retired philosophy professor who found the park a comfortable place where she could reflect and enjoy the company of anyone interested in visiting with her and her dog.

Persons happening to listen in on the three conversing would hear stimulating questions and answers that continued for several weeks. Priscilla found the boy and girl to be intelligent, and actually interested in the big questions of life - so she began to enjoy their questions, and the opportunity to respond to them.

She let the two take the lead in bringing up concerns that they had about what they did or didn't believe. Mark cautiously mentioned how the guys that he knew, didn't really get into talking about such stuff, weren't sure about what they believed, or really didn't care.

Priscilla said, " That sounds familiar. I had gone through that bit. Someone once said this, which was about where I was at back then.

'For the present I do not know what I believe. I might be described as a tourist in the religious landscape.'

"The whole business got very confusing for me. I even felt that people were telling me I should believe this or that. Others confused me. I was hearing even from people who supposedly were well versed in religion. Rather than convince me of anything, they actually did the opposite. I wasn't the only one who felt that way. I read about an incident where a minister thought he had preached well on atheism. After he asked a farmer what he thought of his sermon. Well, the farmer said, "You said a lot, and no doubt it was very clever, but I still believe there is a God ! "

Beth asked, "Priscilla do you believe in God too?"

Priscilla answered, "Yes, it would be harder not to."

"How so?" Beth looked puzzled.

Priscilla said, "I once had a student, who like many others , scoffed at the idea of believing in a God. He even went one further saying,

'I think when you're dead, you're dead and that's all there is to it.'

"I answered him, 'Then you're an atheist.'

'No, I don't believe in that either.' "

"Now that's weird," Mark said.

"That's true, but that way of thinking is quite common among both atheists and agnostics."

"Agnostics?" Mark asked.

Priscilla went on to explain, "Some people, called agnostics, aren't sure if there is a God. Then there are the atheists. Many things have been said about them. For instance,

"An atheist is a person who has no visible means of

support.

"An atheist is one who wishes to God he could believe in God.

The atheist is one who tries to pull God from his throne and in the place of God sets up the phantom chance."

Beth said, "I'm not sure if those glib comments throw much light on the issue."

"Well," said Priscilla, "look at it this way, to be an atheist you need to have more faith in believing in nothing then what it takes to believe in a God. Also, try giving up on believing. You'll find there is no acceptable alternative. For you can't believe against something. You can only believe in it. So you see it doesn't make sense to say, 'I don't believe in God.'

"Now, if you want to ' sit on the fence,' so to speak, and say, 'Yes, I do believe there may be a God. I'm just not sure' - then you'd have caught yourself in a bind. For to say that 'I am an agnostic' is a contradiction. Why? Because we all believe in something ! Emptiness remains only for a moment , and no longer.

One day a person bumps into a friend who is a believer. Her friend asks, ' Is it true you no longer believe?' Her friend says,

'God forgive me, I'm an atheist now.'

The fact that he included 'God' in this way indicates he must still believe in the existence of God.

What's wrong with an atheist's line of thinking can be summed up in this statement.

An atheist cannot find God for the same reason a thief cannot find a policeman.

One other problem that atheists and even agnostics have is this. They are so preoccupied with looking in the most unlikely places to find truth. It's so easy to limit one's view of the world.

One poet put it this way,

'The world is not a prison house but a kind of spiritual kindergarten where millions of bewildered infants are trying to spell ' God ' with the wrong blocks .' anon

Sometimes we can be fooled by false representations of reality and miss the real thing."

"Yes I know what you mean there," Beth said. "I read this story, and remembered it because of my travels with my family in England and in Europe.
There was a street in England that offered a surprise to anyone who was really with it, and kept their eyes open, and stayed alert in their travels   There was something on that street that appeared to be what it was not."

"A house?" Mark asked.

"Yes, a house, but it didn't look like any other house on the block. You know why? " asked Beth.

"No."

"Nobody ever went in or came out of that house, There wasn't a doorbell, nor a letter box. No one ever sat on its balcony."

"The house must have been derelict, ready to be demolished and replaced by a condo or two," Mark guessed.

"No, that wasn't it," Beth responded.

"Thousands of people pass the strange house every day. In the last six decades or so, its estimated that more than a million people have walked by without noticing that house was a sham. It was a dummy house. It's door and windows were painted on a cement wall. Behind that movie- like stage set facade was nothing except a network of girders, some train tracks and a no longer used tunnel entrance. Every so often someone slapped on a fresh coat of paint on the walls to keep it looking like one of the building on the street.
'The House that wasn't ' was put up by the London's Metropolitan Railway. It had been decided it would be the best way to hide the tunnel entrance and fill the gap in the row of houses so as not to spoil the harmonious look of the

street." anon

"I think I get it," said Mark, "Maybe, when an atheist gets so insistent on a no-belief, he stubbornly refuses to budge from that position he's dug in with his heels, and so can't see what's so obvious."

"Yes, that could be," said Beth, "But maybe an atheist has a point. I remember in one of my religious classes, one of my teachers wrote on the board this - if I can remember it right ...
"If a person tells me that he has a car which can do two hundred kms. in one hour, I'd tell him to bring out the car and prove it. If you tell me that there's a God, I'd ask you to produce God to prove God's existence.
"How would you answer that person? Then, he got us in table groups to discuss that and come up with an answer."

"So, did you come up with am answer?"
"We came up with some, but I can't remember if any one of them was the right one."
"Priscilla, what do you think? asked Mark.
"Mark, Beth, I don't think that anyone can claim to know God, nor would one want to know God in that way. The philosopher's view is that you cannot know anything to perfection, especially a God. What I think a believer does not say is, ' I know God,' or ' I see God', or 'I think there is a God.' A believer can legitimately say instead, 'I believe in God!' "

"How so?" asked Mark.
"Beth piped in, "Mark, you're always using that, How so?"
"Well," Mark said impatiently, "I want to know how that all works."

Priscilla injected, "Right Mark, by asking the how

question can lead to what I'm going to say next, namely - we can only know God, by what God does. Moreover, when one says 'I believe in God.' I think what that person is saying, and rightfully so, is this. 'I believe in God, because I believe that God won't let me down.' "

"Kind of like my teammates on our football team - we believe in each other. No one is going to let the other down. We all believe in each other and have confidence in each other," Mark nodded with approval of what he had just said.

Beth stared at Mark for some time. He began to look uncomfortable. Then she turned to Priscilla, saying, "There's got to be more to it than that! When I was in Sunday School- that's a long time ago - I memorized,
'Now we know only in part.. But when perfection comes, our partial knowledge will be abolished. Now we see dimly, as in a dark mirror. Then we will know completely, as we are known now. '
I'm not sure where that's in Bible. But it is."
"First Corinthians, somewhere," said Mark.
"You know that one," Beth asked.
"I've heard of it." Mark stared out across the lake.
"Well, maybe we can't say for sure that we know all there is to know- for sure- till..." Beth paused... "till the end - even maybe then..."

Priscilla also stared across the lake, then all around her, then, looking down at her dog said, " Belief, in something, God, perhaps that's where we need start, a leap of faith. Could it be that, when all is going well, we as creatures, forget about the Creator. In time, we forget God, and eventually may dismiss God as irrelevant or none existent. But when life take different turns, as life inevitably does, then our tune often changes? Maybe we can't even decide that we believe for sure, despite all that we've said, until our faith is tested. Maybe that's when we have a chance to see whether what we cling to stands the test. C.S. Lewis put it this way,

" You never know how much you really believe in anything until its truth or falsehood becomes a matter of life and death. It is easy to say you believe a rope to be strong and sound as long as you are merely using it to cord a box. But supposed you had to hang by that rope over a precipice. Wouldn't you then first discover how much you really trusted it ? Only a real risk tests the reality of a belief."

" But," Mark asked, "If you're talking about belief in that arena, then do we have to wait for a life and death moment to check to see if our belief is for real? I mean, look, doubting can be a painful business - doubting in oneself, doubting in someone else that we are counting on - doubting in someone greater than ourselves - especially when we're up against it, and nowhere else to turn. That's painful, but it's not necessarily a life threatening moment. But then again, I'm thinking the thing to do is to go ahead and believe in God till proven otherwise. It's less painful, and, besides, atheism, or agnosticism doesn't seem the way to go from a practical point of view."

Priscilla said, "That's right Mark, you got it. Atheism won't ease that kind of anxiety you're thinking of, any more than it can provide a refuge in the storms of life or rob death of its sting. When we're young in years, and feel invincible, death doesn't even enter our minds. It's then that your observation rings even more true. For it's easy to flirt with atheism, only dropping it when we're in the presence of death. No wonder one writer noted,

"I buried my materialism in the grave of my father."

Priscilla shifted gears a bit and said," Let's suppose you don't have to wait to test the legitimacy of your belief in God. Maybe there is another way to talk about a belief in God, that has to be about being PRACTICAL . Otherwise, POOF..."

"What?" both Mark, and Beth stared at Priscilla.

Priscilla said, "How's that for getting your attention. Worked with my U students too. Anyway, G.K. Chesterton once said, 'It is often supposed that when people stop believing in God, they believe in nothing. Alas, it's worse than that. When they stop believing in God, they believe in anything. Ours is an age of vast unbelief, and yet an age which is almost pathetically willing to believe in anything, given half a chance."

In a play by Chekov called the "Three Sisters" Act 11: A person called Masha says; 'I think a human being has got to have some faith, or a least he's got to seek faith. Otherwise his life will be empty, empty... How can you live and not know why the cranes fly, why children are born, why the stars shine in the sky... You must either know why you live, or else...nothing matters...everything's just wild grass. "

Having shared those great thinkers' ideas, Priscilla asked her two friends, "What do you think of all that?"

"Maybe, it's being practical to believe in God. Otherwise we lose by default if we believe in nothing," said Mark.

"That's right," said Beth, "and not to believe is running away from the big important questions that nature poses."

"I think you're both on the right track," Priscilla said, patting her dog's head. " What do you think Plato, they're very bright, right!" Turning then to the two with a smile, she went on to say, "I think that together, after our thought wondering and wandering, we're getting closer to where we want to be."

"Right," said Mark, "something like those geese circling there, looking for a place to land after having been foraging out in the grain fields."

"Something like that, right Priscilla?" Beth commented.

"Close. How about we read through some passages that I brought along - Gosh, sorry for a moment I thought I was back in the lecture room. Anyway, maybe you'd be willing to indulge me, by going along with the three of us taking turns reading each of these passages - it may take us more than one meeting together this week-and then after, if you wish, talking about them whenever you happened to be passing through the park in the future. What do you think?"

Mark said, "Sure, that works for me."
"Great, let's do that," Beth added.

" Thanks, you two. Here they are then."

" After an astronomer concluded a lecture on the Milky Way, a person asked him;
" If the world is so little and the universe is so great, can we really believe that God pays any attention to us ? "
" That," replied the astronomer, " depends entirely on how big a God you believe in." anon

Einstein surprised his fans when asked; ' Do you believe that absolutely everything can be expressed scientifically?'
" Yes," he replied, "it would be possible, but it would make no sense. It would be description without meaning- as if you described a Beethoven symphony as variations of wave pressure." anon

When one finally sees the futility of pursuing material wealth or creature comforts or satiating of ones appetites, that person looks elsewhere and discovers God was there all the time, ignored, but very real.

"A person gave up agnosticism and found his way into a place of worship. "I wanted to know the answer of good and evil; what was unbearable was to think that there is no moral awakening, that we creep from moment to moment deceiving ourselves, sometimes guilty and remorseful, sometimes happy, but never knowing the answer, never seeing things as a whole." anon

"Seeing the immense design of the world, she exclaimed one image of wonder mirrored by another image of wonder- the pattern of fern and of feather echoed by the frost on the windowpane, the six rays of the snowflake mirrored by the rock crystal's six rayed eternity. Then she asked herself,
Were those shapes moulded by blindness ?
Who, then, shall teach me doubt ?" Edith Sitwell

"What can be more foolish than to think that all this rare fabric of heaven and earth could come by chance, when all the skill of art is not able to make an oyster? To see rare effects, and no cause; a motion, without a mover; a circle without a centre, a time without an eternity, a second , without a first." anon

"The experience of life nearly always works toward the confirmation of faith. It is the total significance of life that reveals God to humans; and life only can do this; neither thought, nor demonstration, nor miracle, but only life , weaving its threads of daily toil and trial and joy into a pattern on which, at last, is inscribed the name of God."
T.T. Munger

"Don't close all the doors on belief just yet. Live a little more, experience much, and you will eventually discover a God who has been walking with you all the time. You just may not have known it, for if neither intellect and logic or the wonders of creation won't convince you that there is a living God, experience will!" anon

The following week after they had read through the passages, Beth and Mark entered the park in great expectation of meeting their mentor. They were very excited and had so much that they wanted to share. Shakespeare's Hamlet's "To be or not to be..." had taken on so much more meaning! They looked down the path searching for the familiar figure of Priscilla sitting with her dog Plato.
But... they weren't there. The park bench was empty.

The newspaper obituary read, "Priscilla..."

A Goose Island Park bench plaque reads,

"In memory of Priscilla and Plato'
1 Corinthians 13

28

A Week's Worth of Words to Live By

When the onlooker was in his loud, pimply, awkward teens he suffered boils for which his mother had the very cure - poultices containing powerful stuff that he'd rather not know about. All that he wanted to know was, did it work? Would it bring to a head that which troubled, and draw out the dregs, clearing the way for healing? It did!

This onlooker, reflecting deeply on what he absorbed through his senses on his frequent park visits, recalled that experience. He saw the power of the park in its own more spiritually, elevating way also bringing forth from the depths of his being what needed attention to bring about restoration.

When all had come forth as memories, ideas, and responses to nature all around him, and his belief that he was part and parcel of all that is was reaffirmed, he resolved to continue his frequent journeys around Goose Island Park Lake.

He devised a liturgy that, though much of which was not his own, would help him feel that he belonged to something much greater than himself. He could not remember where he got a particular "seven words to live by" theme, but he would take the liberty of using it as a vehicle to enhance his liturgy in motion. "Live, Love, Learn, Laugh, Give, Try and Think" were the words.   anon source

He would reflect and ponder over one per day as he made his way around the park's lake.

During his first week's liturgical walks these thoughts and ideas surfaced, and varied according to the theme for each day.

LIVE was his Sunday walk reflection.

The medical doctor, musician, and missionary Dr. Schweitzer once wrote that people should have "Reverence for life." Exactly what does that mean? In one of Thornton Wilder's plays a woman died. But she was allowed to choose one day to live over again. She chose her 12th birthday. It was then that she savoured and enjoyed everything around her. She said, "you can't look at everything hard enough." To her mother she said in desperation, "Let's really look at one another." Looking around her she also said,
" Earth, you're too wonderful to realize! "
    She discovered that she had missed a lot while living.
    When Alberta's Indian Chief Crowfoot lay dying, he delivered this message to his tribe. " A little while and Crowfoot will be gone from among you. What is life ? It is as the flash of a firefly in the night. It is as the breath of a buffalo in the wintertime. It is as the little shadow that runs across the grass and loses itself in the sunset. "
    In a book entitled "The Touch of the Earth" the writer suggested it's important to not have one's life all blocked out,

not to have the days and weeks totally organized. It's essential to leave gaps and interludes for spontaneous action. Why? Because it is often in those moments when we open ourselves to new unlimited opportunities brought into our lives by chance. It's often then that our life paths take their most interesting turnings. That doesn't mean we should not visit our favourite haunts.

The famous cellist Pablo Cascals, even at age 93, knew the importance of taking time for himself. He said,
"For the past 80 years I have started each day this way. It's not a mechanical routine but something essential to my daily life. I go to the piano. I play two preludes and fugues of Bach's. It's a sort of rediscovery of the world of which I have the joy of being a part. It fills me with awareness of the wonder of life, with a feeling of the incredible marvel of being human. The music is never the same for me, never. Each day it is something new, fantastic and unbelievable. Live each moment of our life while taking in our surroundings."

I regret that I didn't do that when I attended university Grad school. When I graduated, I said to my wife, What wonderful surroundings we live in! Her valid comment was, "You've just noticed? No wonder, you've had your nose buried in your books." She was right ! In my struggle to survive academically, I missed so much! In our struggle to survive or just get through the day, what are we missing?

LOVE - Monday

Let's live. Let's also love. Why? A wise physician once said, "I have been practising medicine for 30 years. I have prescribed many things. But in the long run I have learned that for the most of what ails the human creature the best medicine is love."

Someone then asked him,
"What if it doesn't work? "
He replied, " Double the dose !"

Merely believing as a person of faith is not enough. The word "credo" does not solve the crossword puzzle unless we add the word "amo," I love, in which Jesus summed up his gospel. " Love one another " - how much, how long, how far? - "as I have loved you." There is the measure, the standard Jesus set.

One person wrote, "Love isn't like a reservoir. You'll never drain it dry. It's much more like a natural spring. The longer and the further it flows, the stronger, the deeper and the clearer it becomes. "

The practice of loving is made up of consistent unselfish acts. Remember that Bible passage in 1 Corinthians 13: 5,6?

The fact is that " Love isn't eternal; it's day to day. It brings home the bacon and fries it. It wipes noses. It makes the bed." Sometimes it's even tough love. We love when we engage in the messy stuff of life for others. We can do that when we accept that God first loved us.

LEARN - Tuesday

Live, Love, Learn. It's sad that many people are brought up to think that learning is a duty. Watch a baby learn to walk. The child obviously finds it exciting. The child is simply doing what one is designed to do as we also are designed to do. Yet still we may ask, Why learn anyway ?

The answer ?
We learn to be at peace with ourselves.
We learn what effect we have on other people.
We learn so that we will have minds open to new experiences.

A very learned person once said,
"There are three great questions in life we need answer

over and over. Is it right or wrong? Is it true or false? Is it beautiful or ugly?

Also to learn to know ourselves is to know where we fit into the world, to know what little thing we can give it, to know how very much it can give to us. But that learning process takes effort.

TRY - Wednesday

It can only happen when we try. There is no sense thinking we're going to learn life's lessons if we are afraid to get our feet wet. During a water-safety course a swimming instructor received this note from a worried mother: " My daughter will not be going swimming to the pool until she learns to swim."
We aren't going to go far in our faith journey unless we take the plunge and risk. It is true that some folks are as frightened of learning new things about their faith as they are about risking new challenges. It's then that other Christians need to help them.

Thomas Aquinas, who knew a lot about learning, once said something like this: When you want to get a person to consider your point of view you need to go over to where he is standing, take him by the hand (mentally speaking) and guide him. You don't stand across the room and shout at him; you don't call him a dummy; you don't order him to come to where you are. You start where he is, and work from that position. That's the only way for him to budge. Jesus did that with each of his disciples.

We may respond with: That's easy to say, but wait till you're old and grey!
The actress Sophia Loren, among many others, had an answer to that. She said, "I see myself as very fortunate living now when age isn't that much of a factor.

"So if you put on weight, find that you need glasses, get a little pain in your knee, notice a few brown spots on your hands, don't despair. There is a fountain of youth; it's in your mind, your talents, the creativity of people you love. When you learn to tap this source, you will truly have defeated age."

Do you agree? It is true of course that, as we see more and more years pass, we find it seems that we are confronted with learning more and more to keep on the same spot.

During a discussion in an adult Bible class the conversation drifted to the question of academic education versus on-the-job training. When a young doctor said he had learned as much since leaving school as he did in college, an auto mechanic next to him remarked,

"Yes, Doc, but it's a little simpler for you than it is in my business- you have only two models to work on ! "

Well, that's not quite true. Like any of us, the doctor also needed to give attention to his Christian faith, a challenging learning experience for us all.

LAUGH - Thursday

Accept that we need to Live, Love, Learn , Try, Laugh. Laughter is very good for the health. Today's doctors tell us a good laugh is a great exercise.

" When you explode into laughter your diaphragm descends deep into your body and your lungs expand. This greatly increases the amount of oxygen being taken in. As it expands sideways, the diaphragm gives your heart a gentle rhythmic message. The heart beats faster and harder. Circulation speeds up. Liver, stomach, pancreas, spleen and gall bladder are all stimulated. Your circulation system, your entire system gets an invigorating lift. All of which confirms what Aristotle said 2000 years ago. Laughter is a bodily exercise precious to your health. " anon

GIVE - Friday

We need to Live, Love, Learn, Try, Laugh, and Give. Sometimes it may be a simple act of kindness. But each is important.

"Albert Schweitzer lived and taught in Strasbourg, Germany. One day he and his friends sat together for a meal. It came to the dessert. The waitress brought a big cake to the table. Schweitzer counted the people around the table. There were nine. But Schweitzer cut ten pieces. Ten pieces when they were only nine ? Yes. ' One piece for the young lady who graciously served us,' he explained, handing the extra piece to the waitress." anon

THINK - Saturday- to contemplate on during the walk around the lake.

Let us Live, Love, Learn, Laugh, Try, Give and Think- how our lives can affect not only other people, but also nature's creatures - and how our sensitivity to nature in our life's journey can also profoundly affect us.

The onlooker's visits to the park continued, and his life was enriched by his liturgical walks, and sensitivity to the gifts that nature offers there.

POSTSCRIPT

"Glory be to God for dappled things-
For skies of couple-colour as a brinded cow;
For rose-moles all in stipple upon trout that swim;
Fresh-firecoal chestnut-falls; finches' wings;
Landscape plotted and pieced-fold, fallow,
and plough;
And all trades, their gear and tackle and trim.

All things counter, original, spare, strange;
Whatever is fickle, flecked (who knows how?)
With swift, slow; sweet, sour; adazzle, dim;
He fathers-forth whose beauty is past change:
Praise him."
     Gerald Manley Hopkins 1844-1889

References Cited

1. William Cullan Bryant in Thanatopsis
2. " " " "
3. James Dent
4. Splender, Steven
5. Psalm 104:1-24
6. unknown
7. unknown
8. Bruce Lansky
9. William Wordsworth
10. Gardner Dickinson
11. unknown
12. John Muir
13. Hal Borland
14. John Muir
15. Ann Dillard
16. Bill Vaughan
17. Isaac Walton
18. John Muir
19. Watching Birds by Pasquier p 4
20. Huston Smith
21. George Santayana
22. Watching Birds by Pasquier p 4
23. Lethbridge Community College
24. Watching Birds by Pasquier p 61
25. unknown
26. Ralph Waldo Emerson
27. Pasquier, Watching Birds p 60
28. Pasquier, Watching Birds p 132, 133
29. Pasquier, Watching Birds p 136
30. Pasquier, Watching Birds p 133
31. Pasquier, Watching Birds p 133
32. Pasquier, Watching Birds p 13
33. George Graham Vest, Eulogy of a Dog
34. Joussel
35. A. De Lamartine
36. A.V. Le Reus de Lincy
37. Samuel Butler
38. John Steinbeck

39 John Ruskin
40 Lois Sabin
41 Roger Caras
42 Madison Julius Cawein in Penetralia
43 Jean Paul Richter
    "Flower, Fruit, and Thorn Pieces ch. V111
44 Ernest Hemingway
45 Marvel Brown
46 The Beaver "Rag and Bone Men"
47 "   " p 25, 26 Dec/Jan 2004/05 Zeneta Baker
48 George Santayana
49 Chel Carson
50 John Paul
51 Thenaeus in Deipnosophists x111
52 Kennedy
53 Abraham Sutzkever
    Re Prince Leopold of Belguim & George 3rd
54 Lillian Smith
55 Jean Rostand
56 Al Lee
57 Liz Murray
58 Soren Kierkegaard
59 Thomas Szasz
60 Sir John Lubbock
61 unknown
62 Han Christian Anderson
63 Wilhelm von Humbolt
64 Tom Robbins
65 Albert Camus
66 Ralph Waldo Emerson
67 Henry Fuseli
68 Alan Wilson Watts
69 Margaret Mead
70 Havelock Ellis
71 Dogan
72 Alan Hayhamess
73 Madison Julius Cawein in Penetralia

Bibliography

Baker, Benita, "Rag and Bone Men", The Beaver,
    p 24,-26 December 2004/January 2005
Cliche' Site. com
    "Cliche's, euphemisms,& Figures of Speech, 2004
City of Lethbridge, Henderson Park,
    Park's Dept. Web page, 05/12/2004
Crassweller, Ken, Let Ookpiks Fly,
    One Canadian's Experience
    Trafford Publishing, Victoria, 2004
Crassweller, Ken, The Overturned Canoe,
    Trafford Publishing, Victoria, 2004
Japanese Gardens for North America web page 08/12/2004
Lethbridge Community College,
    "Environmental Science Students solve murder mystery"
    Derik Bly, Communication Coordinator,
    December 5, 2003
Lethbridge and District Japanese Garden Society,
    Nikka Yuko Japanese Garden Brochure, 2004
Murray, Liz., A Brilliant Homeless Teen Who Got a Scholarship to an Ivy League School
Pasquier, Roger F. Watching Birds
    An Introduction to Ornithology,
    Houghton Mifflin Co. Boston, 1977
Splender, Steven, 1909 Poems number 17, pub 1935

Index

numbers indicate chapters

Alcott, Louisa May 22
amo 28
Aquinas , Thomas 28
Aristotle 28
Atheist, Agnostic 27
Baldwin, Faith 21
Bible 1 Corinthians 13: 4-7 27, 28
Bible, Ecclesiastes 3:1-15 15
Bible Genesis 2:18 21
Birds facts 11
Byron, Lord 22
Cascals, Pablo 28
Chekov, Three Sisters 27
Chesterton, G.K. 27
Chief Crowfoot 28
Cowper, Hymn writer 27
credo 28
Defoe D. 21
dogs 13
Douglas, Lloyd C. White Banner 27
eagle 8
Einstein 27
Frankl, Victor 19
God 27
Goodans, R. The River 22
Graham, Billy 21
Happiness 22
Hemingway, Ernest 14
Henderson Lake Park, Lethbridge , Alberta 1
Herophilus, ancient Greek 20
Hopkins, Gerald Manley Postscript
International Dry-Farming Congress 1912 1
Jesus 28
Kennedy, Gerald, clergyman 22
Kurushimu, definition: pain, suffer, struggle 20
Lacombe, John, Alphabetical List of Old Occupations 5,6
Lethbridge, Alberta 1

Lewis, C.S. Author 27
Loneliness, solution to 21
Loren, Sophia 28
love 28
Magritte, Rene, artist 21
Marose, Dora Farm stories 17
McDonald, Coleman 'Once Upon a Little Town' 15
Miller, Arthur 'Death of a Salesman' 21
Munch, Edward , artist 21
Munger TT 27
Nikka Yuko Japanese Gardens 4
Peanuts Linus from cartoon 23
Piners (labourer) 5,6
Russell, Bertrand 22
St. Maria Buffy 23
Schweitzer, Albert 28
Scott, Sir. Walter 22
Seven Words to Live By anon 28
Sitwell, Edith 27
Tooker, George, artist 21
Touch of the Earth anon 29
Tournier, Dr. Paul 21
Vander Post, Lauren The Heart of the Hunter 24
W.W. 11 Canada 3
W.W. 11 England 2
Wilder, Thorton 22, 28
Williams, Tennessee, Orpheus Descending 21
    "   "   The Glass Menagerie 21

By the Same Author

Let Ookpiks Fly

He was an adolescent with "itchy feet" who knew only one thing, that is, get out of Regina, go north and hunt, fish, and maybe trap. So he hitchhiked to La Ronge. That began, through the 1950's and '70's, a unique Canadian cluster of experiences; trading with the Hudson's Bay Company, teaching Native and Inuit (Eskimo) children in the High Arctic, discovering an alternative view of Indian Residential Schools; working with Inuit artists and craftspeople, and preparing for work in community and regional planning. This ended with the question, "what now and to what end?" Meet the author and the characters he learned from. Come away from this, exposed to different perspectives than the conventional ones, having heard from someone like yourself who sought identity, purpose, and spiritual meaning.

The Overturned Canoe

Join in a journey, begin with a prairie boy's search for meaning, Do what kids did, walk wooden sidewalks, cross dirt streets, build rafts and drown out gophers, Throw down your bike, and on your back, see pictures in clouds Skate on the road to the snow banked rink and toast you toes on the oven door. Grow up sucking the juices of life, and eventually surprise your self and neighbours as a sky pilot sharing with others joys and sorrows of life, Between the beginning and the end enter the often unspoken reality of a Canadian minister.

Here Comes the Bus
On the Bus to Banff and Back

If ever there is a survival handbook for riding a bus, then this is it.
If ever there is our world presented in a small package, then
this is it.
If ever there is a celebration and appreciation of all who play a vital part in getting folks safely to their destinations using highways, then this is it.
If ever there is an insider's look at the secrets behind bus riding and bus operations,
 then this is it.
If ever there is true picture of Canadians rubbing shoulders with each other, and with visitors,
then this is it.
This is where the rubber hits the road.
So come along for a bus ride to Banff and back.

The Author

Ken Crassweller: was born in Regina, Saskatchewan, Canada. He. climbed poles for Sask. Telephone Company, worked for the Hudson's Bay Co. Fur Trade in northern Saskatchewan and Manitoba, taught Indian and Inuit children in northern Manitoba, Northern Quebec and on Ellesmere Island, Northwest Territories. He once operated a HBC camp trade. Later he served with Industry and Development, of the Federal Government Northern Affairs in Fort Chimo, Quebec, Iqaluit (Frobisher Bay), in Ottawa, and with the Gov't. of the NWT, in Yellowknife.

Over those years he traveled the Arctic, sharing in the providing of material, financial and technical assistance to the Inuit (Eskimo) artists, carvers, and crafts people.

He earned a B Ed at the University of British Columbia in Art Education, and an MA, in Community and Regional Planning with an emphasis on Arctic Settlements. He once served as principal of an Indian Band run-school in Northern Sask and also earned a degree from St. Andrew's College in Saskatoon, Sask. After ordination in the United Church of Canada, he served churches in Manitoba; Saskatchewan, British Columbia, and Alberta, Canada. He and his life long married partner are blessed with three adult children.

ISBN 1-41205396-X